Accelerated Learning

Learn Any Skill Improve Your Memory Double Your Reading Speed

(Advanced Strategies for Improved Memorization Effective Listening and Increased Productivity)

Thomas Parker

Published By **Phil Dawson**

Thomas Parker

Accelerated Learning: Learn Any Skill Improve Your Memory Double Your Reading Speed (Advanced Strategies for Improved Memorization Effective Listening and Increased Productivity)

ISBN 978-1-998927-86-9

No part of this guidebook shall be reproduced in any form without permission in writing from the publisher except in the case of brief quotations embodied in critical articles or reviews.

Legal & Disclaimer

The information contained in this book is not designed to replace or take the place of any form of medicine or professional medical advice. The information in this book has been provided for educational & entertainment purposes only.

The information contained in this book has been compiled from sources deemed reliable, and it is accurate to the best of the Author's knowledge; however, the Author cannot guarantee its accuracy and validity and cannot be held liable for any errors or omissions. Changes are periodically made to this book. You must consult your doctor or get professional medical advice before using any of the suggested remedies, techniques, or information in this book.

Table Of Contents

Chapter 1: The Perfect Learning Environment

A applicable gaining knowledge of environment isn't something to be underestimated: it allows you to make the maximum from your opportunity to have a take a look at. A learning environment is someplace you enjoy steady and undistracted. Such a place may be your school room, home, or check vicinity. You may be thinking, "How am I alleged to create a splendid mastering environment within the classroom? Isn't that the teacher's interest?" The surroundings additionally includes the people within it, so sure, you could help make a better analyzing surroundings as a scholar. There are 9 traits all appropriate reading environments percentage:

•Always ask questions, regardless of how silly it could sound. Being capable of ask a question is crucial to make the maximum out of a gaining knowledge of consultation. It shows you have got got a herbal hobby and a choice to have a observe. Many people typically have a tendency to avoid asking questions due to the fact they do now not want to appear uneducated, or they think their query is too dumb to be sincerely well well worth an answer, however this can not be in addition from the truth. Geniuses are inquisitive and always curious because of the fact it is the single, brilliant manner of studying. Many of the arena's high-quality thinkers requested now not anything but questions. Albert Einstein posed the query "What can also the universe look like if I rode via it on a beam of mild?", and this precipitated the concept of relativity. Isaac Newton posed the question "Why does an apple fall from a tree?", and this introduced about the law of gravity. Charles Darwin posed the query "Why do the Galapagos islands have such some of species now not decided a few other place?", and this brought approximately the precept of evolution. Value Questions over solutions. As previously said, there can be no such element as a horrific question, and once in a while, the query may not immediately have an answer. The answer may additionally moreover furthermore come days, weeks, months after the query is asked. The question won't honestly have a solution, however the mere act of thinking brings fee because you are exploring the issue; there can be a slight threat you may carry up a query this is by no means been idea of earlier than. When that takes region, the difficulty certainly receives extra thrilling. Remember, discoveries are based totally upon questions, no longer solutions.

•Think divergently. Divergent questioning lets in the arrival of diverse mind about a subject. To think divergently, you need to be organized to break down the concern into small, possible components so each difficulty of the mission can be analyzed independently. A technique used to generate thoughts from divergent assets is brainstorming, a technique that involves generating a list of thoughts from a couple of property in an unstructured way. No concept want to be rejected in a brainstorm due to the reality despite the fact that the idea might not appear potential, it is able to branch off into plausible new thoughts.

•Use a widespread shape of studying fashions. Sometimes you can need to update up the manner you examine. This may be done with the useful resource of the use of a large shape of getting to know models. For instance, at the identical time as analyzing approximately a modern-day programming language, you need to avoid gaining knowledge of actually via a textbook. The textbook can be preceding. You'll want to exchange it up with the aid of the use of performing some on line research at the language, asking a peer and studying from them, doing a little experimentation via coding yourself. Using a vast type of mastering models prevents you from getting burned out and can maintain the state of affairs interesting and appealing.

•Think actual-international eventualities. When you're studying, it's far critical to connect the studying cloth to the real international. Learning approximately a fiction novel? Try connecting the characters to humans you recognize. Good memories usually have practicable characters that fall below an archetype. Sometimes those fictional characters can be related to actual-life humans and can help you have a look at extra approximately them.

•Personalize your reading to fit the standards. You need to increase a getting to know approach that makes the maximum sense for the material you're studying. If you're gaining knowledge of about a pastime, you would need to prioritize exercise and physical gaining knowledge of over theoretical studying. If you are reading approximately era together with chemistry, you would love to have as lots seen or auditory analyzing as viable, however moreover throw in more than one realistic commands. Tailor your mastering technique on your concern.

•Be chronic in your evaluation. After each studying consultation, ask yourself, "what have I observed? What I nevertheless want to take a look at?" Admit if you have struggled to apprehend a subject, don't forget the reason for your conflict and the way you can conquer it to your next analyzing session. Test yourself periodically. Find a listing of questions you discover tough and try to answer them. Found the questions too difficult? Keep on training. Found it too smooth? Find greater difficult questions. Get comments from peers or mentors. What they are capable to tell must be handled like gold.

•The aim for success need to be transparent. You want to continually have a plan. Whether it's miles to have the brilliant grade among your pals or it's getting your dream activity. The path in the course of your intention need to be smooth, and also you want to recognize what it takes to acquire it.

•Ensure you've got were given loads of opportunities to exercise. The very last tool for studying is exercise, and you should ensure you deliver yourself as many alternatives as possible to exercise. There are many strategies to do this. Surround your self with humans who've an interest in the difficulty you need to analyze. You will discover that their information of the trouble will glaringly disregard on you. The first-rate manner to fish is to surround your self with a fisherman. You moreover want to provide your self time to practice. Get into the addiction of scheduling your week so that you have sufficient time to practice.

•Keep your surroundings tidy. No one need's to gaining knowledge of in a disorganized, chaotic mess. Keeping your environment neat and organized will assist you cognizance on your research: a smooth room consequences in a clean mind.

Bringing those kinds of characteristics together will make certain your learning environment is as exceptional as feasible. Be wonderful you keep those in thoughts, and you could discover your capability to learn how to growth immensely.

The Brain and Learning

Learning how your brain learns may be pretty useful to discover your preferred approach of gaining knowledge of.

First, we are able to cover some basics of the brain. The thoughts incorporates about 86 billion nerve cells, moreover referred to as neurons. A nerve mobile receives records from other nerve cells or sensory organs and sends information to different nerve cells. The most massive a part of the human mind is the cerebrum, which makes up eighty 5 percentage of the mind's weight. The cerebrum is split into two elements. The corpus collosum connects each. Strangely sufficient, the left hemisphere controls the right element of the body, and the right hemisphere controls the left issue of the frame. The brain's left hemisphere handles logical obligations, together with studying, writing, talking, and arithmetic facts. The brain's right aspect handles more innovative responsibilities, together with visible notion, pattern recognition, tune, and emotional expression.

People may be left or proper-mind dominant, similar to they may be left and right-hand dominant. A person who's "left-brained" is said to be greater logical, analytical, and goal. A individual who is "right-brained" is stated to be more thoughtful, intuitive, and subjective. As it appears, the idea of left mind and right thoughts dominance is definitely a psychology myth that grew from observations of the human mind which have been dramatically distorted. But it is thrilling how this myth is still extensively famous irrespective of being debunked. Nonetheless, know-how your strengths and weaknesses will assist you to make bigger better strategies of studying. For example, if you discover it hard to take note of a lecture, it would help write down what's being said and compare your notes.

So how does your mind research? To solution that query, one need to be familiar with plasticity or, to be extra precise, neuroplasticity. Neuroplasticity is the thoughts's functionality to exchange and grow subsequently of lifestyles. Learning makes our mind trade physically with the aid of strengthening its neural connections, in addition to developing new connections. Imagine you are analyzing a manner to play the guitar for the number one time ever. Your thoughts has its work lessen out for it. It has to method all of your senses—what you revel in, pay attention and be aware. You could be thinking about all topics to want to be considering playing the guitar. Your motor talents may be placed to the check looking for to thread the guitar. You may be being attentive to your tune and the way the sounds coincide along side your decide actions. Your mind might be storing unique timings and co-ordinates the actions need. Your thoughts may be growing new neural connections to memorize musical actions higher. Everything is going simultaneously internal your thoughts without you even knowledge it. The first couple of instances you select out up the guitar, you are positive to make a few mistakes. But with exercising, your mind will extend and enhance neural connections committed to gambling the guitar. The greater your practice, the stronger the neural connection turns into until you in the long run draw near the art work of playing the guitar. This is how mastering is completed.

There are a few belongings you ought to realize approximately the brain to make the most out of your gaining knowledge of training, if you want to help boost up the neural strengthening of your mind. Humans are visual creatures; we rely on the imaginative and prescient the most out of all of our senses. So, it makes feel that human beings device visual information the excellent. This is because the thoughts has hundreds of neurons dedicated to visible processing. Around 30 percentage of the neurons in the cortex are completely devoted to processing seen statistics. That's a big chew of your thoughts devoted to processing the statistics from your eyes. Humans also are susceptible to motion; we've developed that way to avoid being ambushed through predators. Today we do no longer want to fear approximately being preyed upon through ambush predators, but we still have a keen sense for motion.

We generally tend to forget about about little information. When you're mastering some thing new, getting too caught up within the records and getting crushed is straightforward. A manner to keep away from this is to take a look at the large photo. When you are reading new statistics, the mind may moreover overlook things if it cannot find in advance knowledge to some aspect relatable. When you see it as a whole, it offers your mind some element to head returned and relate to while processing new facts. There's a metaphor that assist you to visualize this concept. Imagine your mind is kind of a closet of shelves; as you add extra clothes, they top off extra of the shelf, and you categorize them. If you upload new information, which include a black sweater, it may pass on the black shelf, wintry weather shelf, or sweater shelf.

Common Mistakes People Make

On Food, Water, and Learning

Food, water, and mastering are related.

The brain's power all comes from glucose, it is the crucial unit of food. Water is likewise important for the mind to art work. Water is crucial for our cells' functioning, and without proper vitamins, our cells will now not function properly. Therefore, a loss of enough water can result in terrible highbrow functioning and a loss of making plans and manage.

In this circumstance, this is because of a metabolic sickness this is generally genetic, kids do now not have enough glucose or water.

In the absence of good enough oxygen to the thoughts tissue or insufficient blood drift to the head, fine areas of the mind can grow to be broken. These areas are answerable for thinking and studying. If this harm is large enough, it can bring about everlasting disability or maybe lack of lifestyles.

Having a excellent healthy dietweight-reduction plan is vital for this circumstance to be averted. It is important people devour enough fluids, which might be critical for correctly thoughts functioning.

Many substances which can be useful to highbrow capability and studying are all clearly present in the additives we consume; as a stop result consuming a balanced food regimen is sure to have an effect on studying. If vitamins is insufficient, terrible effects like awful reminiscence can arise. The brain moreover calls for water. The brain is more than eighty percentage water.

Dehydration can severely impair gaining knowledge of, and most effective growing the amount of water you drink can be sufficient to make a massive distinction in your capability to study.

It's not simply the schooling that makes learning effective—it's also the way .

Scientists have studied the link among water consumption and reading for extra than a decade, and the effects are clean: "Water is crucial to brain characteristic," says Dr. Coyle. "If you do no longer get sufficient water into your thoughts, you can go through." When we consider it, it's far apparent: If we did not drink water, our brains would speedy come to be dehydrated, and we would begin to act like a sponge. We ought to prevent thinking genuinely. We should turn out to be careworn. And our reminiscence would not characteristic as nicely because it want to. Drinking loads of water is one of the most vital subjects we are able to do to maintain our brains wholesome and our reminiscences sharp.

Stop Multitasking

Many people are having hassle with studying because of multitasking (dealing with multiple undertaking at the equal time). Most humans observe with their attention generally being divided with the useful aid of chatting, texting, jogging a blog, and Web browsing, which continuously disrupt the neuroplastic conditions essential to make those studies change right into a synaptic trade in the mind.

Without the lasting structural changes inside the brain, no lengthy-time period mastering can arise. Not only is multitasking an obstacle to reading, but it could furthermore cause the discharge of pressure hormones consisting of cortisol and adrenaline. Chronically excessive stages of cortisol were related to extended aggression and impulsivity and absence of short-time period memory. In different terms, multitasking can put on us down, causing confusion, fatigue, and inflexibility. To assemble lasting impressions on it, your thoughts wants to be targeted.

Remember, we said earlier that a person's strolling reminiscence may additionally need to maintain handiest amongst and seven considered one of a type pictures at one time. This manner that that specialize in a couple of complex project is in reality no longer feasible.

Focusing particularly takes vicinity within the parietal lobes (placed simply at the back of the frontal lobes), which hose down extraneous interest to permit the mind to pay interest on one aspect and then each other. The parietal lobes encompass affiliation regions and are critical to being able to transfer between duties.

What seems like multitasking is virtually moving among multiple responsibilities from side to side, lowering overall performance and growing errors by means of manner of as a good deal as 50 percent.

Gender Differences in Multitasking

It's moreover important you apprehend gender variations exist whilst it gets to humans's capability to multitask. During mind development, a place of the mind that develops greater all of sudden in women than in boys is the occipital lobe. Because of this occipital lobe, women can absorb greater records at a time than boys. This extra sensory attention in women outcomes in an capability to address more facts than boys. They can be a part of up and apprehend extra incoming information and respond because of this.

As ladies turn into women, they increase with this capability. This permits women so that it will carry out multiple responsibilities at one time than men are in all likelihood capable of doing, however this doesn't propose that multitasking even as engaged in a cognitive undertaking like reading will yield no awful effects, reminiscence may be impaired. Avoid multitasking whilst analyzing.

What Happens When You Focus on a Single Task?

When we popularity intensely on a venture handy neurons fireside collectively and they connect to every different. This is known as the Hebbian regulation, named after the Canadian Neuropsychologist Donald Hebb, a pioneer in associative studying.

He first used this phrase in 1949 to give an explanation for how pathways within the thoughts are everyday and strengthened via repetition. Every concept, feeling, movement, and physical sensation triggers masses of neurons, which form a neural community. The extra the brain does a particular task, the stronger the neural community turns into, making the approach more green every successive time. This is why mind maps are very effective in cultivating a very good reminiscence because of the reality they structurally mimic the brain's neural networks, consequently making it more recognizable

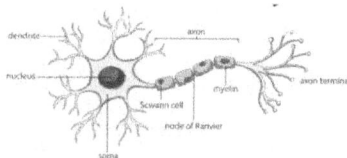

to the mind.

Focus Breeds Insight

Years decrease again, in a conventional have a observe of animal behavior, a chimpanzee changed into given bamboo poles, neither of which emerge as lengthy sufficient to collect a few give up end result placed out of doors its cage. Being thoughtful long enough, plus the choice for those surrender result, the chimpanzee modified into inspired and focused sufficient to attach the 2 brief poles collectively to make an extended pole and reached the fruit outside its cage.

This type of studying is referred to as notion, a tool wherein an animal or person makes use of beyond stories and specializes in the existing challenge handy to reply to a modern situation in a modern manner. Researchers have located that awareness breeds belief. It consequences in new methods of doing topics, and considering an awful lot of human gaining knowledge of is through insight, individuals who are not focused enough have a propensity not to analyze rapid sufficient.

The Reticular Activating System

At the bottom of your thoughts is located the reticular activating mechanism. A form of features are accountable for it, however the one we want to talk about proper right here is called filtering. This is the mechanism that involves a selection what you end up aware of, what stays for your thoughts's foreground, and what sincerely falls into your unconscious recesses.

At any 2d, your thoughts is swamped with loads of hundreds of bits of information streaming into your brain—most of which you cannot attend to, nor do you want to. Because your thoughts want to procedure these information, your RAS makes short judgments approximately what it want to and want to now not see.

Once you're made aware of some thing, like improving in a selected vicinity of your teachers, and once you attention your mind on it, your thoughts stops filtering ways that will help you thrive academically, and filtered records are all of sudden seen. That's why while you grow to be interested in a few component, you start to see it spherical extra often; it isn't always that they have come to be extra frequent round you. It's clearly that your RAS (Reticular Activating System) no longer ignores them.

If you discover ways to hobby on the identical time as studying, your RAS will become greater open to mind you typically do not observe in advance than, in an effort to result in a higher information of necessities and effectiveness within the manner readable consider is inspired upon your memory.

An early 20th-century study observed that the not unusual individual who learns textbook material (without memory strategies) recalls splendid the subsequent:

- After 1 day: fifty four percentage.

- After 7 days: 35 percentage.

- After 14 days: 21 percentage.

- After 21 days: 19 percentage.

- After 28 days: 18 percentage.

Suppose the not unusual pupil recalls simplest 18 percent in their paintings after a 28-day tour. In that case, the subsequent lecturer or instructor simplest has 18 percentage of the vintage statistics to build new information. This way the common organisation or pupil loses eighty percentage of the data (or 80 cents out of each training dollar) after 28 days.

If you analyze your information in a centered time body, you boom bear in thoughts. If you repeat it 10 minutes after reading the records, it will stay for your reminiscence for at the least an hour. Besides, the number one assessment must be completed backward.

You have found out that the best way to decorate is to cast off some thing that stops you from improving. So, you obtain rid of the obstacles like excuses, limiting ideals, and multitasking, and you then surely definately have end up inclined to examine greater. Then you determined out a manner to beautify through the SEE principle of creativeness.

How to Master the Art of Taking Smart Notes

To enhance your studying, taking super notes plays an vital position. Taking notes isn't quite tons paying attention to a lecture and writing down what you observed is pertinent. First, you have to prepare your self for the imminent lecture.

How do you try this? You ask.

You skim over or perhaps have a look at absolutely what the lecture may be over. Sure, this could appear redundant to you, but it's far not. No lecturer can pass over each element of what the text has in it. But you could study the text first to get the gist of the problem. Then, whilst you pay attention the terms popping out of someone's mouth, you may gain more expertise of that scenario. Plus, you can recognize better what you want to pay attention to and what you already apprehend nicely sufficient now not to trouble with.

For instance, let's consider which you are already nicely versed within the venture of conjugating verbs. You do now not need to pay interest or observe every special word about that. But what you do not know a detail about is dissecting sentences. So, you can want to take notes on that. By analyzing approximately the trouble first, being attentive to a person communicate about it subsequent, then writing it down, zero.33, you may cement that into your mind.

Before you head off to the lecture corridor, make certain you've got what you can want to take first rate notes. You will need your computer in some instances. You will constantly want pens and/or pencils. Highlighters are constantly a amazing idea to have too. What else may want to you want to supply with you?

How about a paper or a notepad? How approximately headphones to take note of tune in case you become bored? Nah!

You want to be ready to concentrate cautiously to the lecturer. If you skip in with a bored thoughts-set, you can not expect to get a brilliant deal out of what all and sundry says. Plus, you won't care about taking notes that will help you research the cloth this is being prolonged beyond over.

Now onto sustenance while inside the lecture hall. Coffee is taken into consideration the vintage standby, however caffeine can do topics to your body and thoughts that don't do automatically advocate you could have the exceptional attention.

Try taking a bottle of water in vicinity of a big mocha latte with double espresso images and the sugar content material material of a whole chocolate cake. Water will hold you hydrated and not focusing on how dry your mouth is and what kind of longer you need to be in the lecture hall. Plus, it may now not affect your temper, your frame's capability to sit despite the fact that, nor your mind's capability to pay hobby. It's a win, win, win!

Before you pass into the lecture hall, make sure you've placed some element sustainable into your stomach. You do no longer want to start having a pipe dream about pizza whilst in search of to interest.

Leave the sugary snacks out. Put some trouble at the way to last into your stomach. Nuts, stop give up result, cheeses, and lean meats are splendid. Put a snack together and devour it in advance than stepping into your beauty or lecture hall. There are even lots of snack options you may locate at the shop that encompass everything you need for a few factor with protein, carbs, and the right forms of fat to assist decrease that urge for food for some time, and your tummy may not growl embarrassingly every.

Mindset plays an essential feature. It's important to get a extraordinary relaxation in advance than managing your day in case you want it to be powerful.

The vital detail proper right here is to get into the proper mind-set. Attitude is the whole lot!

Okay, so that you've had been given a terrific night time time time's sleep. You ate a wholesome, filling snack too. You did not devour any coffee or unique caffeine, so you're relax, loose, cushty, and characteristic your bottle of water reachable. Your backpack has all of the necessities you may need, and also you, my buddy, are geared up to rock.

You get into the lecture corridor or the school room; you take your seat, get out your pad of paper and a pen, and are keen on analyzing extra approximately this task you've got study up on. And proper off the bat, you be conscious the lecturer touches on something he'd touched on in a prior lecture.

What do you do? Should you forget about what he is stated? He did say it already, regardless of the whole lot.

No manner. If it is vital sufficient for him to reiterate it, then you definately absolutely had better write that down. Anything this is repeated could probable very well be critical, so keep your ears open for repetition and write it down, even if you have notes. Structuring your notes is excessive. There are unique approaches to do that, so select out what works exceptional for you. Outlining your notes might in all likelihood paintings high-quality for you, it does for plenty people.

You may additionally do that via manner of studying the cloth ahead of time and making an define of it. Check out the critical thing factors within the text and located them on your outline; there should be four or 5 of these key factors most of the time.

Under these key factors, go away place to feature in what the lecturer has to mention on them. You can take notes this manner on paper or on a laptop, something is more comfortable for you.

Another method is called the Cornell Method. In this way, you will use paper to take your notes. First, you will divide your paper into three additives. Make a line down the left issue to block off a small element. Leave the proper aspect massive. Then, at the lowest, draw a line all of the way during. On the left issue, you could write the cues—those would be the key elements of the textual content the lecturer goes over. On the proper aspect, you will write the notes. At the bottom, you may write the summary of the whole lecture. Most lectures summarize on the surrender, besides, making this greater snug with a view to apprehend what to put in writing.

What if you do no longer do properly with notes like that? Then you could do what's known as a thoughts map. This consists of cool animated film-like bubbles that you write information in. Again, it is much like the opportunity way of taking notes, first-class greater visible.

There are though key factors. You will placed those of their non-public bubbles. Off to the sides of these key elements, you can both draw a line to some other bubble, or you could overlap the bubbles to show that what you have got got written is going

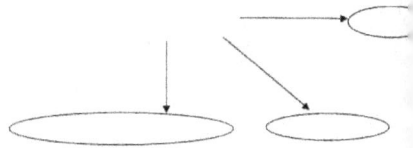

with that key factor.

THE FALL OF ROMAN EMPIREDEBT

IRRESPONSIBLE EMPERORSBARBARIANS

As you may see, every form of word-taking has some form of an outline to begin with. This is an important part of the be conscious-taking approach.

Suppose you have not reviewed the material to be blanketed within the lecture—disgrace on you. But it happens, proper?

Flow notes are okay—not wonderful, not suggested—but you want to do some thing. Just write down what jumps out at you with go with the flow notes. Draw little doodles of things in case you want, make smaller notes below massive texts if you want to. But hold in thoughts that reading these styles of notes, in some time, isn't always clean.

Are You a Visual Learner More Than Anything Else?

Bullet Journaling might be incredible for you. It's photograph, but makes use of the equal concept of an define, however makes it greater fascinating.

You have your key factors and subsequent to them, you have had been given bullet elements in which you jot down the notes that go along with the ones elements. It's plenty less difficult to test off the ones styles of notes too, whether or no longer or now not you are a visual learner.

The fact is that unique topics warrant extremely good techniques to take notes. While data may work better with thoughts mapping notes, and English lectures might be higher if taken within the Cornell technique. Make fine the scenario fits the way you're taking notes.

Lastly, allow's skip over whether you should take notes to your laptop or write them down on paper. Some research have been completed in this controversy. What is thought to be proper is that students who use their laptop systems to take notes generally tend to type within the entirety the speaker says. When tested later, they didn't keep as a good deal of the data as college college students who wrote down the notes on paper.

The motive within the returned of this is that the mind methods statistics better as we write it down, in place of listening and in reality transcribing the lecture.

So, what have we observed out?

• Is there multiple manner to take notes?

a. True

b.False

• Is there simplest one right way for everyone to take notes?

a. True

b.False

• Will a seen learner take higher notes than someone who learns better via listening?

a. Yes

b.No

• Should you take notes the same manner for every situation?

a. Of path

b.No, particular patterns art work fine with high nice topics

•When taking notes, need to you load up on sugar and caffeine?

a. Why no longer?

b.No manner.

•Is it vital to study the cloth earlier than coming to a lecture? Is it vital to have a look at the cloth in advance than attending a convention?

a. Why need to I try this? The instructor is going to inform me the entirety I will need to apprehend.

b.I must continuously take a look at the cloth in advance than going to the lecture, so I could be able to recognize it better and deliver my mind greater opportunities to recognize it.

•Is getting an amazing night time time's sleep important for what you're doing the next day?

a. Not the least bit. What does one day have to do with another?

b.Yes, it topics masses.

•What is better for you, water or espresso?

a. Water

b.Coffee

c. Straight sugar

Exercise: Cornell Method

1.Search on the topic: The inner planets and try to create notes steady with the Cornell

Method. Look at the example beneath:

2.Create a Cornell have a look at-taking approach at the three types which have been lectured. The cause of the look at is to evaluate the three sorts from each other. The first column is wherein the mind are indexed, and the second column is wherein the definitions are indexed.

Exercise: Mind Map Method

1.Create thoughts map notes approximately the importance of the thoughts map word-taking technique.

2.Create a thoughts map be conscious about the bodies of water. You can constantly draw smooth branches into your mind map

Exercise: Bullet Journaling

1.Create a bullet magazine notes approximately your favored TV Series. This method is powerful, in particular if you have authentic drawing capabilities. Open your imaginitive aspect, use special shades and your creativeness! Use solar sun shades, numbers,

Chapter 2: Memory Improvement Techniques

Tips to Remember Anything

According to the Willamette University, "the thoughts in no way loses something." The phenomenon of forgetfulness is often the fabricated from one (or a combination of) these 3:

1.The facts modified into not saved inside the first region.

2.The facts cannot be retrieved.

three.The statistics have emerge as saved but could not be retrieved at the same time as needed.

Obviously, reminiscence works an lousy lot more efficiently on the identical time as energetic in desire to passive. A character need to be triggered and inquisitive about the shop and retrieve facts from their reminiscence efficiently.

There are techniques worried with memory: hobby (storing the statistics) and undergo in thoughts (retrieving the facts). There are a few fundamental pointers concerned with memory formation:

•Focus: It is herbal for human beings to do severa topics proper now, in particular within the occasion that they sense pressed for time. By focusing solely on what you are attempting to have a observe, however, it's miles going to be much less hard to create and shop reminiscence effectively the number one time.

•Association: You can deliver a lift on your reminiscence via associating received data with first rate topics. You also can associate facts with unique imagery or tales. For example, you could partner a wonderful founding father's tale with a movie you have got got visible or a present day movie star newsflash.

•Connections: By growing logical connections, you may in addition decorate your reminiscence. For example, you could be a part of the subjects you've got found out with the useful resource of organizing them proper proper right into a hierarchy or by way of adding new data from outdoor resources. If you're studying bones, try to see how every bone hyperlinks to every specific bone. Try drawing the connections as nicely so you can use each facets of your mind. By activating as many regions of your thoughts as feasible, you beautify reminiscence enter.

It can't be emphasized enough that unique humans test in any other case. However, numerous tips can resource in memory formation. Here are 25 pointers that permit you to keep in mind a few element.

1.Analyze your fabric proper after a lecture or proper after reading it. It may additionally furthermore seem repetitive to transport over a quarter after you have got simply completed analyzing it, however this permits you to slim down vital factors of the communicate and pass back to any questions you can have written down.

2.Make certain to get your facts right the first time. It is frequently difficult to update wrong facts with the proper one.

3.Minimize or eliminate distractions earlier than you even begin reading. This includes internal (having a pipe dream, making to-do lists) and outdoor distractions (own family, buddies, TV). If you locate this hard, use the checkmark machine. Each time you locate yourself distracted, test a bit of paper. Count the checks on the forestall of your session and set a intention to reduce them on your next consultation.

4.Understand the cloth in location of honestly memorizing its contents. Read in advance than splendor, ask questions once they upward push up, and supply an explanation for the mind to a look at pal to make clear your information.

5.Don't do the whole thing at once. Space out your examine schooling however have a have a look at frequently. Focus on one difficulty count each time. This way, you could resultseasily hold facts to your lengthy-term memory.

6.Having a "messy table" at some point of studying is a component of contention for loads—some cannot have a look at with muddle, even as others do no longer mind it in any respect. The essential hassle is you have got all of your check substances internal clean attain if you need to crosscheck your notes, facts, or memory.

7.Find a quiet, cushty location to take a look at that is not your mattress. Studying in mattress (or maybe on your mattress room) sends blended signs in your mind, which might also contribute to sleepiness while you are tired.

8.Take short, common breaks. Experiments say that human minds are greater able to remembering topics that rise up at the start and on the prevent of reviewing than what you have were given determined out at the end. Taking breaks is like having separate cue cards for separate topics.

nine.Move. A sedentary body makes a sleepy mind. Besides, blood flow tends to pool at your ft when you have been sitting too prolonged. Aside from feasible health risks, this imposes lots much less blood turns into to be had to feed power on your mind, so that you end up sleepy or unfocused.

10. If you want to have a look at with a set, select oldsters that are severe about reading. Their momentum may in truth inspire you to tempo up you're studying. At the very least, you can get some new thoughts about the lesson from them.

eleven. Do not stress your frame to live up even as you are cramming a few thing. Try studying within the afternoon, early night time, or morning (in case you are a morning person). Sleep is critical in reminiscence formation, and a few aspect you take a look at on the identical time as sleep deprived can also moreover definitely as nicely were thrown out the window.

12. Avoid being attentive to song on the equal time as you take a look at because of the truth this is often a form of distraction. If you have to, attempt taking note of instrumental tune as an alternative.

thirteen. Use your emotions to connect to the trendy information that you studies. For instance, World War II caused 1945. To recollect the 12 months I be a part of the amount forty five emerge as the age I sincerely have my 1/3 little one. Therefore, each time there can be a question on even as World War II surrender become, I will take into account my ultimate little one and my age and come up with the answer 1945.

14. Chunk statistics. Classify them into some crucial necessities, then paintings on the thoughts determined below every one of them—going from fashionable to unique. For instance, you want to bear in mind eleven digits, 18329008756. You can spoil these numbers into chunks, consisting of 1–832–900–8756. This can be tons less complicated to bear in thoughts. Memory is restricted, but you could increase this restrict in case you prepare mind.

15. Use/create mnemonics as a device for chunking quite centered data. This may be inside the shape of abbreviations, like PEMDAS for the order of operations in algebra, or in the shape of terms or sentences, like "each specific boy does great" to represent the strains of a musical group of workers (EGBDF). Be certain to memorize it simply and efficaciously whilst you undergo in mind that even a small

mistakes may additionally additionally throw you off course.

sixteen. "Go to the extremes" at the same time as making your mnemonic. A licensure examination professor as quickly as stated that students regularly recollect styles of mnemonics extremely good: (1) those involving humor, and (2) people with a rude or even sexual connotation. The extra photograph the imagery, the less difficult it's going to possibly be to preserve it in your reminiscence.

17. Choose a peg from which you can dangle your facts on. It can be a few aspect from a rhyme, a series, or perhaps your Grandma's antique socks! For example, you may equate the specific regions of the thoughts to the unique patches you determined on granny's socks.

18. If you stay/have a have a examine with any man or woman, placed on a few thing to clue them in at the same time as you do

no longer need to be disturbed. It might be earphones (whether or not or now not you may pay attention to track is your preference), a baseball cap, and masses of others.

19. Have a "worry pad" close by in case you all of sudden have stray mind or go through in thoughts an errand—but do not act on it. You may moreover additionally whole the ones personal responsibilities after you end reading or finally of your check break.

20. Test your knowledge. You can do that on the give up of each web page, or on the forestall of a particular facts-dense material. Analyze new terms and vintage approaches, then relate them to new records you have taken in. For example, on the cease of each internet web page, near your eyes and consider what you surely have study. Try to don't forget keywords and connect to the modern day information.

21. Maximize the usage of your senses. Although you could have a favored gaining information of favor, speaking about it, drawing it, writing it, or performing it out will create greater avenues to your thoughts to retrieve the information you need to preserve. For instance, at the same time as you visit beauty for a lecture, you observe the PowerPoint slides; you pay interest the records, write or take notes, which lets in you memorize better and maintain better.

22. "Erase to take into account." Try the use of a pencil or a board to write down down everything you want to don't forget, then pass over the list at the same time as you are completed reviewing. Progressively erase devices as rapid as you correctly retained them in your memory.

23. Use your mind to assume or provide you with a story with new records that will help you recall. For instance, some additives of a cell include the plasma membrane (additionally called the cellular wall to allow

tremendous fluids and chemicals into and out of the cellular), and the nucleus (the control center of the mobile hobby). You can use your imagination to offer you a tale along with a captain on a deliver call Nucleus manipulate every issue of the supply. Its ship is produced from metallic referred to as the Plasma membrane allows prevent water from moving into the deliver.

24. Give your photo location and motion to make it greater incredible. You can use body actions or maybe additives of your body as cues to recall records. For instance, you can soar your finger on the knuckles and regions of your unique hand to recollect which calendar months have 30 or 31 days.

25. Use symbols to encode facts. For instance, you may use the French flag to endure in mind the right order of colours in a specific chemical response.

Making Mnemonics

Okay, so that you understand the way you study top notch, you have got created a have a have a look at plan, you already have your material within the the front of you, and you've got were given a hard concept of approaches you'll pass about your evaluation, then you see a block of things you need to memorize.

According to Mind Tools, a web commercial enterprise agency committed to supplying essential abilties for profession constructing, there are three essential traits to an powerful mnemonic: imagination, association, and location.

Imagination

It has been said time and again that establishments and connections assist fortify recollections. To create those establishments and connections, but, you want a wholesome imagination to visualise some aspect you're reading in a totally distinct scenario. The more potent the photo—whether a single image, a story, or a smooth phrase—the longer the reminiscence will live with you. It additionally turns into much less hard to retrieve them as time passes. Your imagery can be violent, sensual, and vibrant, anything rocks your boat—for as extended as it enables you go through in thoughts.

Don't be afraid to test! You no longer often create a single mnemonic from a flash of genius. You will regularly undergo numerous thoughts earlier than you can pick a unmarried modern one if you want to provide you with the feel of "Yes, I'm a genius."

Chapter 3: Association

You need to hyperlink what you are analyzing with some thing else. There are severa manner of making establishments. Some are:

•Mashing matters together.

•Merging images.

•Rotating statistics.

•Linking gadgets based totally totally on coloration, shape, feeling, and so on.

For instance, clinical college students use not unusual gadgets—which includes boots, sun shades, and lemons—to provide an explanation for the normal and atypical shapes of positive organs in x-ray imagery.

Location

You can use vicinity in each its physical and intellectual experience. Mentally, setting your mnemonics in fantastic locations gives you a placing from wherein you can location and go through in thoughts certain records with out blending it up with others. Setting your mnemonic of noble gases inside the environment, and your mnemonic of earth alkali metals inside the soil, for instance, lets in you to split the ones chemical substances with out worry of bewilderment.

Physically, you could remember in which you have determined out terrific facts to cause the rush of reminiscences observed at the identical time. This is the attention in the back of mental experiments that say that you need to alternate your have a look at corner on occasion instead of holing up in the library each time.

The Memory Vault

Spaced repetition isn't foolproof. It would now not assure you may bear in mind some component; it genuinely maximizes how properly you can memorize thru passively looking on the cloth over and over.

Visual reminiscence is one-of-a-kind because of the fact you're developing recollections intentionally. When you reread a set of notes, you refresh the facts on your mind. But when you have a have a look at a 7-step machine for your notes, you may have a tough time recreating that listing even a minute whilst you observe it over.

The trouble is you are essentially throwing dust on the wall and hoping for some sticks, and what sticks is what you don't forget. This shotgun-fashion technique works, but it isn't always the best way to do not forget matters as it is not below your manage.

Visual reminiscence is one-of-a-kind. It isn't always clearly active; it's far modern. You turn the facts you are mastering into photographs, and then you virtually definately hold the ones pics to your thoughts. To hold the throwing the dust at the wall metaphor, the use of seen memory is equivalent to placing hooks at the wall after which putting your records onto the hooks so you can get to it every time you need it. Your visible memory is just one among your lively intellectual filing systems.

three Types of Memory

•Passive: you glaringly remember a small quantity of what you listen.

•Active: You take notes, check them again and again, and get in reps.

•Creative: You flip thoughts into images after which hold them for your reminiscence.

Passive is equivalent to sitting at your computer. Active is equal to playing sports. Creativity is equivalent to going to the gym. Each has a great diploma of effect for your capacity to assemble muscle groups and strength.

How Does Memory Work?

All information is relationships.

Your instructor in no way asks you to keep in thoughts the variety 1984, or the decision George Washington, or the shade blue. Instead, you preserve in mind X e-book have become written in 1984, George Washington is the primary President, and Blue is the colour of enterprise business agency. As you can see, each piece of records incorporates as a minimum quantities. Therefore, to take into account statistics, we really want to do not forget relationships. Because relationships are not usually linear, the remarkable way to represent relationships is visible. This is why we are able to maintain close a flowchart, infographic, or mind map extra than a block of text. We like lists and bullet factors due to the truth they arrange information visually.

The thoughts does now not go through in thoughts static symbols, pics, or sounds. Instead, it recollects the patterns or relationships amongst symbols, pictures, and sounds. You apprehend that an apple is an apple because you spot the purple shade, a stem, it is spherical, all the seen, 3d tendencies that mean that it's far an apple. The phrases you examine here are made from letters. Each letter represents a valid. The five letters in apple create a series of sounds, a totally specific relationship of sounds which you have related to a picture of an apple on your thoughts. You have moreover related as much as this photo/sound mixture tastes and smells and textures. All the ones stimuli from the five senses come together to form a aspect called an apple. Feed your mind surely one of these stimuli like simply the flavor, or surely the picture, and all the relaxation of the net of connections is activated.

Because of the manner the thoughts is installation, we are able to create relationships between snap shots loads extra speedy and intuitively than connections among sounds, tastes, or every other experience. We will use this reality to go through in mind extra and studies faster.

How Does Visual Memory Work?

Visual reminiscence is your capability to remember relationships amongst pictures.

It technique that you may inform a person the way to get from your teens residence in your antique excessive college over the phone, even in case you are at the opportunity component of the arena. It method you can tell a person how to get from the the front door of your private home for your bedroom and take preserve of your pockets from the lower once more of the top left drawer of your desk.

You have been the usage of your visible memory your whole lifestyles. The first-class new issue you're gaining knowledge of now's a way to apply this latent capacity to memorize special types of records besides the layout of houses, avenue routes, and desks.

Visual reminiscence can be very considered one in every of a kind out of your verbal memory. Your verbal reminiscence shops vocabulary and pronunciation, but seen reminiscence statistics pages of records. This is because of the fact your eyes step by step memorize records as you touch, study, play with or use it. This imprints styles into your mind that can be diagnosed by means of using using your visible reminiscence.

Visual reminiscence is some element that you use every day without identifying it. You can not explicitly inform a person to memorize via searching at them, however you do that unconsciously whilst you are on foot beyond a cutting-edge region without looking at it. It is just like the manner a infant sees things. Their eyes apprehend styles and memorize the surroundings.

Learning to visualize is kind of like studying the way to have a look at and write, but as an opportunity to the use of letters and numbers, you are using pix. Think of it like getting to know hieroglyphics. Instead of representing a word or idea via a series of letters (which represent sounds), it's far represented via a single photo. The tremendous matters about the use of photographs are that you may offer you with your very very personal symbols, you do not must use any individual else's, so it's far clearly intuitive.

A few tips for visualizing nicely, via an example: Think approximately visualizing just like the use of Photoshop, however in actual existence. You can take any photo out of your "My Pictures" folder and plop it into your contemporary-day 3d truth. Pretty easy, right? Let's say you want to visualise Angelina Jolie sitting during from you at a desk in a restaurant.

Are you going to close your eyes or preserve them open? You have to do both, but do you really want to want to near your eyes on every occasion you want to keep in mind a few element? No. So preserve your eyes open even as you visualize.

Is she going to be existence-size, in reality massive, or surely small? Make her big sufficient to pinnacle off the show.

Is she going to be in colour or black and white? Color is higher. You might not recall the colors as well as the define of her form, however it's miles a extraordinary dependancy to get into because it will make the reminiscence richer.

Is she going to be a 2d cardboard cutout or 3d? Obviously three-d! We want to appearance all her curves, her lips, her hair, and plenty of others.

Do you want to apply a thumbnail photo of her, or a excessive-res photo? The better decision, the higher. Instead of visualizing a vague photograph of the shape of her parent, take into account the manner her hair falls on her shoulders, the cut and coloration, and material of her dress, her heels, her earrings.

What about lighting? When you are doing a photograph shoot, you typically convey in more lighting. Make sure your visualizations are excellent and excessive evaluation.

What else? You aren't slicing pictures out of a newspaper and developing a university out of creation paper and glue. You are a grasp photographer, pc pix expert, and Photoshop prodigy all wrapped up in a single.

Capture each image and scene nicely, add aptitude, motion, explosions, and make it interesting. This is your non-public reminiscence palace, do now not flip it into a monotonous, musty vintage library.

The concept is which you are playing a activity of Pictionary at the side of your destiny self. In normal Pictionary, you draw a image on a whiteboard, and your partner tries to wager what phrase you mean.

With visible reminiscence, you have big advantages. First, you're gambling with yourself, so that you apprehend how you observed. Second, you could create/visualize very amazing and three-D images in no time, in choice to seeking to draw them out through hand. The motive is not to create the appropriate image for every piece of information. It clearly needs to be a hint that is right sufficient to cause your memory in some time.

Using Visual Cues

•Easy, use symbols. Heart = Love, Lion = Courage, Apple = intuitive design.

•Rhyming. George rhymes with porridge. Imaging infant bear retaining a bowl of porridge.

•Acronyms. Minimum Viable Product is going to MVP. Imagine MVP trophy.

•Split up syllables. Mass ache setts turn out to be Mass= church, Achua = Kleenex, setts

= chair. Turn the ones into one image: Angelina Jolie sitting in church in a chair, sneezing proper right right into a Kleenex whilst keeping the field in her lap.

•Sound-a-like. CEO looks like a seal. Imagine Jeff Bezos (CEO of Amazon) swinging via the amazon jungle with a miniature little one seal below his arm. For Jeff use a chef hat, for Bezos use a bay leaf. Have the chef hat with a bay leaf peeking out of the sideband of the hat.

Chapter 4: What about Numbers?

For numbers, we use the Major System. It turns every quantity right right right into a letter. You can then use the letter to provide you an photograph. For example, the range 2 interprets to the letter "N." We pick a phrase that begins with "N," like Newspaper.

Let's say we want to memorize a random reality about Massachusetts: Mass Achua Sits turn out to be the second country to prohibit toddler components gives at maternity hospitals (the primary aspect that got here up once I Googled "MA was the second country to").

The Handshake Method

When palms meet, a courting is shaped. When photos intersect, they will be related, and a dating is common among them.

For instance, to connect a carrot and a truck, make the carrot the equal period due to the truth the truck and feature it speared via the windshield. Add damaged glass flying everywhere to make the scene even extra memorable.

The Road Trip Method

When you circulate in your morning shuttle, you pass the equal houses, bridges, and billboards. You can join an photograph to each of these objects and use the direction to keep the snap shots in order.

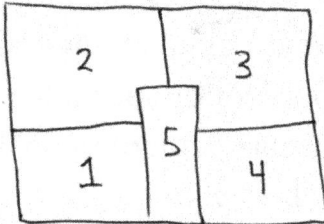

Suppose you preferred to memorize "the seven conduct of surprisingly effective people". In that case, you can join one photograph representing each addiction to every of the seven houses, landmarks, and bridges located on the route from your home on your office, economic institution ATM or church.

The Mansion Method

Turn your home or condominium into a "memory mansion." You can break up your home up into rooms and preserve special sorts of records in each room.

For instance, you can pick 7 gadgets for your mattress room after which use each object as a manner to keep music of what conduct you do on that day of the week. Use each item, like your bed or your table, as a hand (see pinky-swear method) to hold as a good buy as five behavior for that day. If you operate your mattress room for this, you could visualize your week earlier than mattress or whilst you wake up thru clearly looking spherical your room.

The Car Method

You in all likelihood spend time to your car each day. You can use this time to get very familiar with the indoors of your vehicle, and you could use the multitude of things in your vehicle to maintain tune of your every day to-dos.

For example, you could use the dashboard and control console to your automobile to store photographs of what you want to get entire these days.

Photographic Memory

Photographic reminiscence is defined due to the truth the unusual functionality to endure in thoughts, in actual (or nearly actual) element, topics surely as they had been seen. It is an ability that pleasant a small fraction of the population is stated to personal. However, there are definitely numerous topics that any character can do to growth their memory capability. Aside from studying a ebook, one of the splendid techniques to attain this is thru good sized workout. With the eyes, looking at something and remembering it is able to be visible as like working closer to a capability. By doing that, the reminiscence ability of your mind will enhance over the years and turn out to be greater specific. Of route, being able to hold in mind things with out a photo won't sound like a large deal, but it could have a terrific effect at the manner you live your life.

Photographic reminiscence is also referred to as 'Eidetic reminiscence'. 'Eidetic' comes from the Greek root word meaning 'seen' or 'to look.' Some people differentiate amongst photographic and eidetic reminiscences, but for this newsletter, we're capable of deal with the terms identically and interchangeably.

The crucial distinction a number of the terms is that photographic memory refers particularly to the visible, at the equal time as eidetic consists of the opportunity four senses—smell, taste, touch, and sound. Both fall beneath the elegance of typical accrued reminiscence, however we can stay with photographic, as this is the maximum cushty and maximum recognizable word.

There are severa procedures it manifests itself to human beings. Some people file they will be capable of remember an photo, nearly as a picture of their minds, proper down to the smallest, most insignificant detail. It is as although they are sporting an real tough reproduction of the image with them of their arms and can zoom in or out, specializing in intrinsic data. Others have claimed that lets in you to have a take a look at a few issue inner to their mind as if they were looking on the place thru the second pair of eyes. For those human beings, the image glints, reputedly disappearing and reappearing at random. Still, others report that they may one way or the other view the photograph in fact with the useful resource of focusing their awareness on the man or woman or item, taking it in nearly like a seen encompass—but now not quite. They all appear like slightly awesome approaches of viewing the same component.

Individuals from time to time say that the scene is so smooth and realistic that the image seems now not in fact of their minds however as something that they truly see with their eyes. Sometimes, it's far skilled as almost a flashback, plunging the man or woman proper again into an revel in. Or it's also defined as a filmstrip walking parallel to truth in order that the individual sees each proper now. As this shape of reminiscence can arise involuntarily, it's far sometimes visible as a miles much much less desirable example of not unusual amassed memory skills. Despite this, the term remains frequently used as a defining function of the capability. However, the individual will commonly truely "see it"—the scene isn't in reality there to look, as plenty as it is to "be visible," and therefore, there may be no visible detail to witness. This isn't always the same as the revel in of viewing or analyzing some element or dreaming.

Other times of photographic reminiscence consist of not genuinely pictures but words and/or numbers. For instance, some humans can look over an unknown textual content for a few minutes, then recite it lower again verbatim or almost verbatim. This also can be carried out with mathematical equations alongside aspect memorizing the digits of Pi or rankings of numbers beyond the decimal.

Memory has 3 styles of approaches which might be encoding the records, maintaining the information, and recalling the records. The thoughts will first accumulate the brand new records and then make an effort to collate the information into an encoded piece of latest statistics. Then the thoughts uses that records and way to categorise and maintain the info of the new statistics. Eventually, the mind remembers the statistics whilst and in case you ever want it.

Many components of the mind are worried in this reminiscence retention machine. The first department entails the cerebral cortex. This division of the mind refers without delay to the outer layer of your mind. This is the region that right now gets new statistics because of an inflow of the senses. Next, you may have the Amygdala, that is designed to highlight the important records and maintain the essential records in your existence. Within a small distance from the Amygdala is the hippocampus, which continues reminiscences stored for later use. Finally, the very last part of the equation is the frontal lobes. Within the ones elements, you may advantage assist in consciously being capable of retrieve the information this is new and has been stored.

There are many benefits to facilitating the development of strong reminiscence talents. Obviously, it's miles seriously essential that you use the ones system for more potent educational and intellectual abilties. To reap university, we should be capable of memorize data and be capable of endure in mind it at will for assessments and papers. Improved reminiscence and recollection skills lead proper away to progressed grades and prolonged check overall performance. Being capable of arrange and prioritize obligations in addition to staying targeted on the mission available, while infinite interruptions and distractions occur, is a vital trouble of improved studying. In our personal lives, the potential to keep in mind humans, activities, and appointments will make a huge difference in our potential to hold a success relationships and navigate the headaches of existence.

You can be capable of manage your life extra gently and efficaciously. No greater worrying freak-outs at the same time as you are on foot late and can't find out your car keys. Sometimes we are able to enter a room, mins later, we don't have any concept why we went in. Besides, there may be the very simple reality that that is the right vicinity wherein all of our reminiscences from our lives are saved. At the surrender of the day, no longer anything can ever be extra valuable than our reminiscences, and it's far up to you if you want to keep at once to them and they remain clean, smooth, and without troubles available. Other blessings of a very good reminiscence encompass extended self guarantee because you not want to worry being embarrassed, with the intention to offer a discount in pressure and tension. If you want to make your thoughts up, there may be a miles extra threat that you will maintain in mind what you made a decision months later. It turns into tons less tough to analyze new competencies, you will be able to process quick what you study and be capable of take this new information and positioned it into motion a whole lot quicker. If you are someone who has loads of hassle making selections, that is worth it. You can also even absolutely have extra a laugh because of the fact you may endure in mind a lot greater of your existence. You can be capable of appearance lower lower back and undergo in mind while you had been more youthful and harmless. There is probably hundreds much less while you ever overlook experiencing it because of the fact you in no way forgot it first of all. You can also be able to do not forget things that have happened which might be important to you, it's going to deliver you greater happiness and in an effort to make you more at ease and could them more efficient.

There is any other method, that is interesting to recognize, with a purpose to growth memory. This is the exercise of exercise at least four hours after analyzing some thing. In a currently published have a observe, researchers placed that placed up-getting to know exercise can enhance the mind's ability to gather new statistics. However, simplest if this is carried out in a manner that is particular to the window of time which you need it. The records you sincerely located out becomes a memory this is lengthy-time period by means of the usage of a machine that requires the release of the chemical substances inner your mind that correlates with workout. These chemical materials are dopamine, BDNF factors for growth, and norepinephrine. According to numerous case research, scientists have located a connection among exercise and the technique of gaining knowledge of. By workout, you will be able to keep more records. However, greater studies is being carried out to assist us apprehend why that is feasible and the manner it affects our thoughts's function for reminiscence retention.

Furthermore, there's no clean manner to why 4 hours of relaxation time after exercise will assist you preserve the facts you genuinely decided. The truth is that we do no longer genuinely apprehend. But scientists realise that humans have intrinsic wants to do topics that exercise will assist them do. The relaxation of the body desires to lighten up after a exercising. If you can relaxation inside 4 hours after a exercising, then you will be pleasant. Make first rate you relaxation at the least four hours after exercise to permit your brain modify, and it will decorate your memory retention. Also, you want to consider that one of the motives for the ones 4 hours of rest time after exercise is to allow your thoughts transition from a physical united states of america of exercising to a chemical nation of relaxation, that is vital to sense well while you sit up to your next exercising day. Another vital element is that you want to use your mind's reminiscence center to bear in mind the facts that you definitely found out. The excellent manner to do that is to use your hands to attempt to hold in mind what you clearly positioned out. That is usually a few thing that human beings exercising. Research is being finished approximately the consequences of mind stimulation on reminiscence retention and additionally on how the brain achieves top highbrow skills.

Memory Palace - Building a Mental Castle for Your Mnemonic Devices

Mnemonic devices are, quite genuinely, equipment that help us take into account. They are based totally on the concept that the extra good sized something is, the a great deal less complicated it's far going to be for us to recall. We are introduced to mnemonics as early as grade university, and people mnemonics can often be recalled properly into past due adulthood, which means that they've served their supposed motive. Here are a few examples:

•Roy G. Biv: The imaginary fellow who reminds you of the colors of the rainbow: red, orange, yellow, green, blue, indigo and violet.

•Please excuse my expensive Aunt Sally: The order of operations for essential linear algebra: parentheses,   exponents, multiplication, department, addition, subtraction.

•Every proper boy deserves fudge: In song idea instructions, the notes on a treble clef: EGBDF.

Anyone who went to a big American desired university may don't forget: In fourteen hundred and 90-, Columbus sailed the ocean blue.

Mnemonics can take many paperwork; they can be acronyms, rhymes, nonsense sentences, bodily pointers, and visualizations. Let's find out them giant to look which techniques can artwork excellent for you. We'll become with analyzing to assemble a memory palace—a highbrow fortress wherein you can store your mnemonic devices for solid-preserving.

Acronyms and Acrostics

The first 3 examples listed above are known as acrostics; the ones are sentences or phrases whose terms start with the equal letter of the terms that want to be memorized. Acrostics art work as mnemonic devices because of the fact the sentences fashioned are nearly continuously contrived and, therefore, stupid or nonsensical. Humorous matters are clean to decide to memory because of the truth we adore to sense actual—maintain in mind those endorphins?

Another instance of acrostic mnemonics is: My very knowledgeable mom sincerely served us noodles—a a laugh sentence to recollect the sun tool: Mercury, Earth, Mars, Venus, Jupiter, Saturn, Uranus, and Neptune. Of direction, in advance than Pluto's demotion, the mom served 9 pizzas!

Acronyms are every different sturdy mnemonic device. The use of acronyms is famous in the naming of companies and businesses. Originally supposed to be a time-saver, it's also grow to be an easy way to bear in mind what the organizations are and what they do. NASA may be an example of this in the American government. In studying, acronyms can help us undergo in mind important data and figures. Here's a couple of examples:

•Mr. Mimal: The man who stands next to the Mississippi River inside the Midwest, in which Minnesota is his hat, Iowa his face, Missouri his torso, Arkansas his legs, and Louisiana his toes (MIMAL). Take a look. You'll discover it simply does resemble someone sporting a chef's hat.

•Homes: Useful acronym for recalling the Great Lakes: Huron, Ontario, Michigan, Erie, and Superior.

You can use acronyms and acrostics to beneficial resource inside the memorization of virtually some thing, and the fine part is attending to create them. The extra amusing you're having, the greater you will examine.

Feel the Rhythm, Feel the Rhyme

We are all familiar with rhymes, specially at the same time as we have been children, beginning with nursery rhymes and children's singsongs. Many children's books rhyme and Dr. Seuss tapped into the cognitive characteristic of rhymes for preschoolers with dozens of classics like the cat inside the hat and inexperienced egg and ham.

Experts have for the reason that set up that adults moreover make a more potent cognitive connection to words and terms after they rhyme, that is one of the motives a few human beings can memorize track lyrics with such ease. But the neuroscience in the again of rhyme can be a beneficial device to assist up keep in thoughts critical facts. The ditty above about Columbus is one little poem and right here are a few more examples:

•Leaves of 3, permit or not it's far: do no longer touch! It's poison ivy!

•Red sun at night time, sailor's pride; the red sun at morning, sailors, take caution: to forecast the weather whilst ships were a number one supply of transportation. Almanacs provide records suggesting this poem is correct.

•Thirty is heat, twenty is first-rate, ten is cool and 0 is ice: a chunk rhyme to help Fahrenheit users don't forget the same Celsius values. 30*C is ready 85 ranges Fahrenheit, while zero ranges Celsius is the equal of 32* F, the thing at which water freezes into ice.

You do now not want to apply present rhymes to use their mnemonic powers. Like with acronyms and acrostics, you can have some a laugh writing your very personal to guide them to all the more memorable.

Chapter 5: You Put a Spell on Me

Spelling mnemonics are quick stupid sentences that allow you to do not forget how to spell a few usually misspelled words. Here are a few examples, but if you have terms you continuously warfare with, have a laugh making up your personal!

•Big elephants can typically apprehend small elephants: To spell 'because of the fact.'

•We listen with our ear: To keep in mind which 'hear' (proper proper right here) to use.

•Never believe a lie: To keep in mind the proper order of the 'i.E., in belief.'

•'I' earlier than 'E', besides after 'C', or at the same time as it looks as if an 'A', as is a neighbor and weigh: Of path, local English audio machine will comprehend there are numerous, many exceptions to this rule, however it's far a tremendous starter mnemonic for younger schoolchildren.

Visualization Mnemonics

Some mnemonics rely on sight instead of sound. These can be matters as easy as imagining the huge variety 8 as a snowman or keeping up your left hand to make an L. When we see subjects that make feel to the visible administering centers of the thoughts, we regularly have an 'aha!' 2d and begin to encode the image for everlasting storage. Here are a few more examples:

•Making a fist to do not forget which months have 31 days: Ball your proper hand into a fist together collectively along with your knuckles dealing with you. Touching the knuckle of your index finger, say 'January', then the dip amongst that knuckle and the subsequent is 'February', middle finger knuckle is 'March', the subsequent dip is 'April', ring finger knuckle is 'May', the dip is 'June', the pinky knuckle is 'July'. Go decrease returned in your index finger knuckle and begin over with 'August', the dip is 'September', middle finger knuckle is 'October', the dip is 'November', ring finger knuckle is 'December'. All the months that fell on a knuckle have 31 days, the dips do no longer.

•Using letters to determine species of camel: There are   kinds of camel, the unmarried-humped Dromedary, and the double-humped Bactrian. To endure in mind which range is which, or choose out that

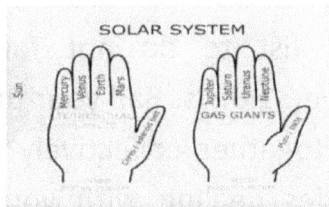

SOLAR SYSTEM

you are looking at, a capital B (for Bactrian) has two humps. A capital D (for Dromedary) has one hump.

Solar System Hand Visual

Another Solar System Mnemonic

The photograph above suggests the way to apply your fingers to memorize the sun device and is a piece greater specific than the planet's acrostic.

Visualization mnemonics are but every other fun device that you can create with. Try to provide you with the cleverest pictures or the nice guidelines that will help you do not forget matters better. Draw your non-public little doodles at the identical time as you are analyzing or make little sketches to hold for your art work area.

Building a Palace for Your Mnemonics

One of the high-quality tactics to apply mnemonic devices is to create a global for them to stay in. Some people name this a memory palace or a reminiscence citadel, or you can use the fancier call 'the technique of loci'. It works like this: You have a positive large quantity of facts you need to memorize or information you need to don't forget sequentially. How are you able to successfully and correctly preserve it so you can present it lower returned nicely? For our instance, we are going to say you are getting equipped an vital speech for paintings, and it desires to be memorized. Let's get began!

•Choose a area to your memory palace: This need to be someplace you are very familiar with, some vicinity like your own home, your dad and mom' home, your place of job, and so forth. You want to pick out someplace the manner round and in that you're feeling comfortable. You'll need with a purpose to see this place even as you shut your eyes. Design a path through that region- you may come in the the the front door, perhaps pass throughout the residence, or to the dwelling room. Make it a direction that makes sense, possibly like your ordinary whilst you get home from art work or faculty. If you cannot take into account the proper course, truly cognizance on going clockwise via the rooms.

•Choose standout skills along your course: If you're tracing the course, you are taking at the identical time as you get domestic you may begin at the aspect of your the the front door. Note special crucial capabilities as you do your walkthrough. The table in which you place your keys and bag is probably your next prevent. Into the mattress room to kick off your footwear will be prevent amount three. Then you may flow into the powder room to clean your face and arms. Next, head to the kitchen to make a snack, and finally, move sit down down at the sofa inside the residing room. You've now marked six constant elements in your memory palace route. Jot them down somewhere. These are going to be the locations wherein you save your reminiscences.

•Encode the route: This is the step in that you are going to dedicate the palace and the course to memory in advance than which include the data you'll keep. If you can, bodily stroll the direction, stopping in all the fixed elements for prolonged sufficient to have a have a have a look at them and do not forget their features. Do highbrow run-throughs till you've got the whole reminiscence palace memorized and can with out difficulty recall all the information of your everyday elements.

•Time to make institutions: Now that your palace is constructed, you can add the statistics you want to need to stay there. Since we're the usage of the instance of memorizing a commercial enterprise speech, allow's join the additives of your speak to the locations in your house and what they stand for:

•Front door: This will constitute the advent to the speech, which you may companion with setting out the door.

•Entry table: This will represent the cause of the speech as you agree on level, which you associate with setting down your own home.

•Bedroom: This will represent that you're snug on the diploma now, and approximately to begin the pork of the speech, which you can associate with setting out your shoes.

•Bathroom: This will constitute that you're starting to smooth up the loose results in your speech, which you could accomplice with washing your face and hands.

•Kitchen: This will characterize your very last thoughts, and supplying acknowledgments, which you can accomplice with getting a chunk snack to close your day.

•Living room couch: This will constitute the perception of your speech, in which you could take a deep breath and loosen up, that you'll companion with setting your feet up for some TV time.

As you begin to join the textual content of your speech to the places for your reminiscence palace, make it exaggerated. Picture your speech introduction as you enter the grandest castle doors. Pretend your access desk can communicate and recites the venture declaration of your speech to you. When you get for your bed room and take your shoes off, have them run themselves to the closet and soar in at the same time as singing your speech to you.

There are countless ways to use mnemonics; you'd be tough-pressed to discover a manner that doesn't aid you, even in some small way, to enhance your reminiscence and your have a study talents.

Exercising Memory Palace

The reminiscence palace became specially utilized by audio system to undergo in mind the crucial issue factors to be made in a speech, in the proper order. Some comparable photo-based totally completely techniques later came to mild and were used for other functions, together with breathing, religious sporting activities, and so on.

In the middle a long term and the Renaissance days, a complicated version of the method of loci advanced, the usage of specifically memorized imaginary areas (Memory Theaters or Palaces) and problematic structures of pre-determined symbolic snap shots, frequently full of non secular or occult connotations.

Do you have were given a residence? A rented condo? No hassle. We are going to apply that residence to memorize 20 gadgets or gadgets.

Now, Pay 100% Attention!!

You drove down and opened the gate to your property or any residence at all you're the usage of. So, the gate isn't any 1. You walked on the ground/tile outside and approached your door.

As you study or pay attention, photo the entirety, the actual residence you're the use of, on your mind like a film. If you're currently in that house, take a walk and bodily range those items as you contact them collectively along with your fingers in real existence.

The tile/floor is variety 2, while the door is range 3. As you bought in, the primary component you located in the living room is a chair. The chair is amount four. Following the order of objects in the dwelling room, the subsequent became an paintings portrait drawing of Nelson Mandela.

Art portrait is quantity five. After art, the following is a tv. TV is variety 6. You seemed up in advance than shifting to the eating and noticed a scarily massive ceiling fan hanging on the ceiling. You looked at it, shook your head 7 times in disbelief at the size, and headed to the dining. The ceiling fan is 7.

You moved to the ingesting and saw an Italian dining table, so our full-size variety eight is a eating desk. The subsequent within the proper path is a nine-deck refrigerator, so our variety 9 is a refrigerator.

You appeared up all over again earlier than heading to the kitchen and noticed this relatively made rotatable 10-one year-vintage Chinese chandelier dangling inside the dining, at the roof, even as pointing without delay at the middle of the desk. The chandelier is our massive range 10.

You entered the kitchen and unknowingly hit your leg at the garbage can because it became too close to the door and all of the dust inner splashed on the floor and you had no preference, however to clean up earlier than persevering with. So, the rubbish can is amount 11.

The subsequent thing you noticed is cooking fuel, 12. You endured searching in that course and located a sink, thirteen, leaking water. The subsequent is a locker, 14, to preserve plates, pots, spoons, and masses of others. You stored looking in sequential order, and you observed an oven sold 15 years ago. So, the oven is variety 15.

Luckily for you, there is a 2nd door that effects in room 1, so you had been given in via that door, and also you observed a king-sized mattress, 16, perfectly designed for sixteen and pregnant teenage girls who love to roll from one fringe of the bed to any other.

Stretching your hand from the mattress, the subsequent your hand touches is an historic lamp, 17. In the equal course, it's miles observed with the aid of using an 18 horsepower (newly invented) air-conditional, 18, near the window. Then a window, 19, built through using Bill Gates at the same time as he changed into 19 years antique and changed into inside the housing and construction business enterprise. After the window is a cloth cloth cabinet 20 full of 20 grimy garments of squaddies from II World War, (2nd). I wonder at the identical time as they stored the ones 20 dirty army uniforms to your cloth cupboard. Maybe your grandfather saved it.

Gladly, the room has a spacious rest room, so you were given inner and saw a twenty first-century washing device, 21, a huge mirror at the wall, 22, hung through the musicians Bruno Mars and Lil Wayne once they were stubborn 22 years antique boys, a big tissue paper, 23, the precept relaxation room itself, 24, and eventually, a tub in sequential order, 25.

Now, we need to analyze times till we dedicate those clean-to-keep in mind places and their numbers into memory. You might imagine it's tough, however it isn't. Let's list them first, then stroll through the adventure all over again and visually spot every object and its associated numbers.

Oh, make sure you have an anchor or a trigger in each multiple of five. This way the numbers five, 10, 15, 20, and so on. Are alleged to have more triggers. This permits in making sure your pics or loci are effects recalled in order.

1.Gate.

2.Outside floor/tile.

three.Door.

4.Chair.

five.Mandela's artwork (Nelson Mandela's 5-year-antique paintings as a little one).

6.TV.

7.Ceiling fan.

8.Table.

nine.Refrigerator.

10. Chandelier (a ten-yr-antique Chinese chandelier).

eleven. Trashcan.

12. Cooking fuel.

thirteen. Sink.

14. Locker.

15. Oven (a 15-twelve months-vintage outdated oven)

16. King-sized mattress.

17. Lamp/moderate.

18. AC (air-conditional).

19. Window.

20. Wardrobe (20 II World War grimy army uniforms).

21. Washing device.

22. Mirror.

23. Tissue paper.

24. Toilet.

25. Bathtub.

Take a moment and walk via this adventure out of your gate to your bath in advance and backward till it turns into 2nd nature.

Always undergo in thoughts your multiples of five anchors to help you navigate effects inside the course of recall.

We shall have an exercise about the memory palace we in reality created to apprehend if you could recollect they all without any hassle in an lousy lot plenty much less than 3 seconds. Don't only answer on my own, however vividly and colorfully see the photo to your thoughts's eyes sitting in that specific place—this is quite critical.

If I ask you which ones of them object is the amount 9, what you want to do is undergo in mind the variety 10 as it stood out and right away assume backward, and also you'll get the range nine.

Or you could keep in thoughts the range five, then skip forward, and you'll get the variety nine. If the variety nine comes proper away to you, then extraordinary— you acquired't want the multiples of five anchor approach in this kind of case. And yes, getting it proper away is what you need.

Test

•Which object is variety 7? _Ceiling fan_ are you high quality about that?

•Which item is #1? _____ are you super about that?

•Which object is quantity 4? _____ are you fine approximately that?

•Which object is large range 21? _____ are you quality about that?

•Which object is big variety five? _____ are you certain about that?

•Which object is big range 3? _____ are you sure about that?

•Which item is quantity 8? _____ are you high-quality approximately that?

•Which item is enormous range 9? _____ are you nice approximately that?

•Which item is range 6? _____ are you extraordinary about that?

•Which item is extensive range 2? _____ are you advantageous about that?

•Which object is range 10? _____ are you extraordinary about that?

•Which item is variety 14? _____ are you best about that?

•Which item is range 15? _____ are you high quality about that?

•Which item is huge range sixteen? _____ are you certain about that?

•Which item is huge range 24? _____ are you certain approximately that?

•Which item is range 17? _____ are you tremendous about that?

•Which item is range 25? _____ are you certain about that?

•Which item is range 18? _____ are you high quality about that?

•Which object is variety eleven? _____ are you sure about that?

•Which item is great range 19? _____ are you certain approximately that?

•Which object is amount 12? _____ are you positive about that?

•Which object is variety thirteen? _____ are you positive approximately that?

•Which item is variety 22? _____ are you positive about that?

•Which object is variety 20? _____
are you effective approximately that?

•Which item is amount 23? _____
are you top notch approximately that?

Finally, you have got internalized your first 25 devices for your first reminiscence palace. You can construct limitless reminiscence palaces if you need, however in this ebook, we'll use the best above.

"What's subsequent?" you asked. The next detail is you're going to memorize the ones 20 objects with 5 extra devices introduced to it in your memory palace, and also you'll undergo in thoughts they all, no longer like in advance than that you weren't capable of don't forget all. With this, you'll see the difference and the manner outstanding your reminiscence is, but you've been neglecting to educate it those form of while.

Here is the listing of those 20 gadgets + 5 greater, 25.

Number 1 is

Chair

Number 2 is

Egg

Number 3 is

Wi-Fi

Number four is

Gate

Number 5 is

Choir

Number 6 is

Smile

Number 7 is

Dictionary

Number eight is

Light

Number nine is

 Swim

Number 10 is

 Cigar

Number eleven is

 Cat

Number 12 is

 Affair

Number thirteen is

 Hairy chest

Number 14 is

 School

Number 15 is

 Water

Number sixteen is

 Pin

Number 17 is

Dance

Number 18 is

Tape

Number 19 is

Thinking

Number 20 is

Amazon

Number 21 is

Laugh

Number 22 is

Gas

Number 23 is

Book

Number 24 is

Selfie

Number 25 is

Dog

Let's get commenced in memorizing these 25 gadgets into our prolonged-time period reminiscence. Use von fuse to make your affiliation first rate, scary, truely silly, outrageous, and impossible.

Chapter 6: This Is How You Memorize

You drove on your gate and have been given irritated, then pulled the chair in your automobile and slammed it on the gate. Sadly, the gate refused to open, so that you ran to all your associates' homes and accumulated their chairs, located them collectively, and climbed it to jump into the compound.

You landed on the ground, however unfortunately, the eggs you stole and hid for your pocket while you have been taking chairs from your buddies' houses popped out of your pocket and splashed at the floor. You're addicted to eggs, and you could't trust dropping quite a few these uncooked eggs, so you went on your knees and commenced licking them dry together with your tongue.

You walked to the door and tried to open it to no avail, so you placed your hand in your pocket and brought out your smartphone soaked in egg yolk, and started looking for a

Wi-Fi network to message someone to send you every other key. Unfortunately, you couldn't find any Wi-Fi while status on the door, so that you angrily slammed your head at the door, and it opened.

Boom, the first trouble you saw is a sofa chair through the factor. The 2nd you preferred to sit down on it, it magically became to an iron gate with sharp items that might pierce through everyone who sits on it. Luckily for you, you have got been brief to leap off from this magical couch that end up a risky gate.

Continue making up stories until the ultimate item. The story is imaginary, and it's not feasible to arise in real life, however bet what? Whatever we can trust, our subconscious mind sees it as reality. So, this story can be recalled as a truth in our mind's eyes, and you may be capable of do not forget the devices on this list.

Revisit this adventure and study the film you've actually created and cement it into your mind that will help you don't forget the whole thing without missing a thing. Analyze is essential to preserve in mind.

There are too many benefits to this adventure device. It will make you come to be more innovative. If you're a author or a scriptwriter, you'll provide you with films most directors will beg you to shop for the right to create proper into a huge-show display movie.

How to Develop Rapid Reading Skills

Do what takes place at the same time as you increase your productiveness? You end up who you've got were given continuously desired to be. I will percent seven brief guidelines with you to enhance your analyzing, starting from in recent times. However, in advance than starting this take a look at, I have to want you to do the following topics:

•Turn off your cellular cellular telephone or placed it in aircraft mode.

•Look for a cushty, quiet, and well-lit region wherein you could consciousness, to soak up the most of this cloth.

•Close your eyes, breathe and exhale five instances, loosen up, and neglect about about a few component you can not do presently.

This manner, you may be better organized to research and be effective.

Avoid Setbacks

Rewards repress analyzing, kill productiveness and annihilate learning. These setbacks rise up on numerous sports and for numerous reasons. Let me quote the 2 maximum common setback conditions.

For example, whilst you start analyzing a totally hard textual content, complete of unexpected phrases and complete of

116

complicated sentences, it is simplest natural which you make setbacks until you may understand the which means of everything this is written.

On the opportunity hand, the second state of affairs is worse and additional commonplace: whilst you have got a have a look at content material material without concentrating, your thoughts can boycott your analyzing and erase every word that has actually been study. So, without cognizance—even though the e-book is easy—its reading will by no means be powerful and you'll be pressured to reread the same sentence numerous times, spending mins searching for to discern out what the hell is written.

However, right proper here is the coolest statistics: I will teach you a manner to clear up every of these demanding situations in reality.

For Academic Articles and Complex Texts

To address complicated texts—those that you regularly want to use the dictionary for and make the setbacks seem inevitable—the hint is straightforward: in preference to looking each new, surprising word, circle phrases that are not clear and glide on.

This will can help you understand the this means that of the textual content with the assist of context. This way, what's going to be written next will permit you to recognize the modern terms, without having to look for a dictionary. This way, you can save time and awareness. Then examine the passage once more.

This time, I assure that you may be able to recognize the message effectively in lots much less time.

For Lack of Concentration

"Just pay attention" the naive reader should say this as though it had been that smooth. It isn't always. In this enjoy, being able to concentrate, study and have a look at efficaciously, may be a actual mission. A efficient take a look at consultation relies upon on numerous factors, which consist of time, mood, affinity with content material material, and so on.

Use a Guide

This tip is nearly to boom pace and avoid setbacks in reading. Take a pencil or a pen to help you at some point of studying. Then use this device to manual literally your eyes among traces and phrases. This manner you will hold your eyes regular at the thing in which they really want to appearance.

Besides, you can keep away from the uncomfortable situation of getting out of place on the equal time as switching traces. Lastly, thru keeping your hobby regular at one point, you'll additionally be training your functionality to pay interest.

Delete Sub-Vocalization

Do that uninteresting voice that repeats each word that has been examine inner your thoughts? This voice has a name, and it is known as sub-vocalization. In this sense, sub-vocalization is the end result of a complicated approach that involves a sequence of things, including:

•The manner we discover ways to observe while we are kids.

•The bodily mechanisms of studying, which incorporates the primary visible cortex and motor, sensory system.

•Tension within the jaw and tongue.

•The lack of specific schooling that teaches analyzing past studying si-lá-bi-ca.

So, I will advise some powerful carrying sports that will help you take away this evil in 3 steps. First, lighten up your neck, jaw, and tongue. Stretch your neck, turn your head to at least one trouble, then the opposite, and look for physical video video games for your facial muscle groups. Next, search for effective strategies to loosen up your mind and reduce your anxieties. Working for your breath is an powerful manner to reduce tension.

Finally, pre-observe the textual content, looking for illustrations, underlined or ambitious phrases. This way you will be able to get a state-of-the-art idea of what studying is about, without worrying about every phrase for my part. Besides, it's miles actually worth remembering that sub-vocalization ends whilst applying dynamic reading strategies.

This is due to the fact the commonplace reader does now not use all the processing strength of his mind in the reading way. And this opens the possibility for the mind to use this idle capacity for other duties, at the side of sub-vocalization. This moreover explains why the common reader with out issues loses his consciousness.

After all, it's miles tough to lose recognition while an activity occupies one hundred% of our minds.

Improve Your Memory

What unique is it to take a look at many books in case you cannot don't forget some thing proper away? Having an top notch reminiscence is critical to the learning approach. In this way, analyzing is absolutely the start of a complicated device of solving the contents on your reminiscence.

Here's a smooth method on the way to beautify your placed up-analyzing gaining knowledge of. But first, I want to introduce you step by step as new facts turns into reminiscences inner our minds.

The Learning Process

Learning through reading starts inside the optical tool, with the purchase of new records through the eyes, collectively with one-of-a-type senses (listening to, touch, heady scent, and flavor). This records is saved for fractions of a 2nd in the sensory reminiscence.

Next, the contents examine are allotted to the walking memory, which has a quick length. So, our mind selects exquisite the maximum crucial reminiscences, that lets in you to be saved there for a chunk longer— at maximum, 3 weeks. Finally, those memories that had been taken into consideration maximum critical are consistent as lengthy-time period reminiscences.

Answer truely: in what type of reminiscence do you need to maintain the content material fabric you invest your precious time studying? If you need your mastering to reveal into lengthy-term recollections, you then actually need to make this method less complex. Thus, it's far crucial to apprehend that recollections are synapses: nerve impulses emitted through their neurons.

The greater stimuli a synapse receives, the stronger the "path" it is going through. In this way, you choose out the memories that allows you to accompany you for the relaxation of your life. But this is a much more complex problem, and that could be a brief precis.

In this way, my maximum sincere indication is the route of have a study and memorization, of professor Renato Alves. A whole, step-with the resource of-step schooling that teaches you the manner to make the maximum of your thoughts's capability—whatever the hobby, and what goals you want.

Without a doubt, this path have to be step one to any education that involves gaining knowledge of: ENEM, lobbies, public contests, OAB examination, and language guides.

High x Low Productivity

Before improving reading capabilities, a splendid reader spends a good deal of time reading oneself. In this enjoy, a honest self-evaluation will display you your personal alternatives.

•Why do you take a look at?

•Which readings do you've got extra affinity for?

•What texts do you want to observe—under a take a look at, examination, or paintings?

Having the ones solutions reachable is a super begin to recognise while you need to have a observe every kind of content material material.

Next, you have to additionally understand what your excessive and espresso productivity moments are. For example, I find out it less complex to pay interest early in the morning once I wake up. First, I take a shower, drink an exceptional coffee, and then I'm willing to observe and feature a have a look at—whatever the content fabric is probably. So, I set apart my mornings for those greater complex readings that require greater of my potential to pay interest. On the opportunity hand, I recognize my productiveness is low earlier than I doze off.

Still, I want to observe something to loosen up my thoughts in advance than I doze off. So, I select a bedside ebook, funnier and much less deep, which goes to be a pride and could help you sleep higher.

Lastly, choosing the proper analyzing for the right time will help you set up your content material call for into your available time extra productively.

Variety

When I have become graduating, despite the reality that the listing of readings appeared endless, I commonly saved an amusement ebook available to clean my thoughts of the heavy contents of university. This helped me to rest my thoughts at the same time as providing stimuli not to hyperlink the dependancy of analyzing with a horrible idea of tiredness. So, I hold this addiction to these days.

I constantly have particular books at my disposal: a theoretical one—to teach me some element approximately the area and its truths—and every other one for my moments of low productivity. In this manner, I assure you that it is viable to stability nicely the look for a modern-day mastering with the want for enjoyment.

Validate Your Readings

The manner of validating new content is one of the simplest techniques to beautify the transformation of latest studying into long-term recollections. The technique that I will display under grow to be provided via the usage of Professor Renato Alves for the number one module of his Course of Study and Memorization.

The method is quite simple, however powerful. It includes 3 steps, which should be repeated in advance than, inside the course of, and after every a success studying.

Step 1—Read with Concentration

Advising to take a look at with cognizance may additionally appear redundant in the starting. But the fact is that maximum students are blind to powerful strategies of attention and memorization. In this feel, starting your studying in a quiet, prepared, well-lit vicinity and mind-freed from any anxiety is the first step to make your take a look at consultation effective. Also, preserving your mobile cellular phone grew to grow to be off - or any device that could interrupt your studies—can save you your studying from being aggravated with out want.

What is your intention? Why do you need it? What motivates you? Regardless of your answers, you could need to focus on Einstein to your next study consultation.

Step 2—Have a Master Attitude

What does it suggest to have a hold close intellectual thoughts-set?

Are you capable of train what you've got surely discovered to someone else? According to Richard Feynman, winner of the 1965 Nobel Prize for Physics, education something to every different person is the extremely good manner to look at. In this feel, if you can educate a complex concept to a little one, then your mastering can be complete.

Step three—Make Yourself Understood

Learning is an internal conversation way. So, endure in mind to be clean with yourself.

After completing every reading, solution the subsequent questions:

•Why is that this reading essential to me?

•What did I clearly test?

•How to arrange this records in my mind?

•What are the connections of this content with other getting to know?

In this way, look for affinity with content material fabric, and make the reading and gaining knowledge of method attractive for you. So, create establishments among what is written and certainly one of a type learnings that are already strong in your mind.

Also, take a look at aloud, and pay attention to your private voice via repeating the most critical passages—which need to be memorized. In this manner, you may be using every other enjoy—the feel of hearing to stimulate the synapses which you need to hold for longer.

Chapter 7: Speed Writing Skills

You will meet some humans on your lifestyles who can as it should be be referred to as writing machines, however do you want to be like them as well? It isn't always that hard as all you want is practice. But writing quicker best for the sake of it's going to not get you a long way. You want to maintain each issue of the content fabric fabric at the identical time as writing at a faster velocity.

•Grammar: In this era in which every body can express themselves on line, the net has modified how people can and cannot communicate. You can choose out to put in writing in informal English at the net, but you may need to understand formal English for all various things in existence, of which grammar is an vital detail.

•Sentence production: Some humans suppose that rules must now not restrict their writing, but tips are supposed to offer your writing an favored essence at the stop of the day. Whatever form of writing you are doing, be it some cutting-edge prose or an informative weblog, the sentence shape is the most vital element. And for that, you need to be aware of the right strategies of sentence creation. Imagine a puzzle in which all of the quantities are arranged within the incorrect way. Does it appear terrific to you? No, right? It is due to the fact the scattered quantities obtained't shape a photograph together, but at the same time as aligned within the proper way, they may appear harmonious and exceptional. The equal is going for a sentence. If the phrases are not well organized, the sentence received't make proper enjoy. So, even in case you are practicing tempo writing, you want to preserve in thoughts that the sentence form cannot be compromised.

•Tense: As you need to already recognize, stressful is some element that conveys the facts of what came about when. Having a dominative information of tenses is crucial to border your sentences in the proper way. Tenses typically can be divided into 3 fundamental kinds - past stressful, gift stressful, and future demanding. Now, those can yet again be further categorized into numerous types. But maximum mistakes in writing are devoted concerning those tenses. You need to be aware about the one-of-a-kind perspectives of grammar, as well. For example, the tenses will variety based totally totally on the situation of being, interest finished, or intending with the interest.

•Singular or plural words: Now, as quickly as I factor out singular or plural, the first concept that consists of anyone's mind is that I am talking about one or many. But that isn't always the fine software program software of those terms. They are also used within the case of project-verb agreement. This is while the verb that you have used within the sentence can be decided based on the vast style of the noun in that identical sentence. If you want to install writing the sentence successfully, you first ought to determine whether the noun is singular or plural. You want to be aware of sure specific instances in which even the plural nouns are handled as singular, which includes "facts". It is probably splendid in case you stored in thoughts that irrespective of the reality that collective nouns may sound like plural nouns, maximum of them are singular. This is because of the fact they may be used to regarding a set of devices wherein the gathering, in itself, is singular. For example, crowd. There are non-countable nouns like 'water.' You can't keep in mind it and therefore, it is constantly handled to be singular.

•Indefinite and specific articles: Articles are utilized in each sentence and they will be additionally an essential element. Even if they may be small, their effect is massive. Their role is continuously preceding a noun. The article's usage is generally to signify whether or now not or no longer the noun is preferred or particular, plural or singular. There are types of articles—indefinite and real. Indefinite articles yet again have bureaucracy—singular (a, an) and plural (some). If you test with some element cutting-edge or speak over with some thing for the first time in your article, you operate an indefinite article. But take into account that 'an' is used within the case of vowels and 'a' in the case of consonants. 'The' is the incredible specific article in English grammar, and it's miles used with every singular and plural nouns. You also can use it with nouns which have already been added in writing before. Choosing the right article, even while velocity writing, is critical to deliver the message nicely.

•Contractions: Contractions are those phrases wherein one or greater letters are dropped to make the phrase shorter. When you write those terms, to make up for the dropped letters, an apostrophe is used. For example, can't, obtained't, they'll, and so on. Now, the usage of contractions isn't usual; they are now not used in formal writing, but on the subject of informal writing, they can be freely used, specifically in instances wherein area is restricted, as an example, advert copies. When it includes regular conversations, human beings use contractions all of the time, and so when you are tempo writing, you might be tempted to use them there as well to store time. But you need to bear in mind the kind of writing that you are doing. If it's miles formal, then contractions are a big no. Also, within the case of informal writing, a colloquial tone can be maintained via using the use of contractions.

•Conjunctive: Conjunctive is a term used to indicate the linking verbs or the 'be' verbs as you normally realize them to be. But there are conjunctive adverbs as properly (as an example, 'consequently,' 'however'), and they may be used to connect incredible mind. Punctuation is of the utmost significance with regards to conjunctive terms.

•Spelling: One of the maximum commonplace mistakes that everyone makes in pace writing involves spellings. And even local audio tool make these mistakes, so that you are not on my own! Your spelling abilties are a few component that you'll be attempting at some stage in your life. You might be able to write fast, but in case your spellings are all incorrect, then there may be no need for what you have were given written. So, in case you want to get your spellings proper, right right here are some pointers which you ought to hold in mind.

•Know the suggestions: There are positive not unusual rules related to spellings in the English Language. Don't take an excessive amount of stress with the resource of the use of seeking to examine they all straight away due to the fact with a view to splendid motive hazard, and you may not be capable of recollect any of them properly. So, the first rate way to understand approximately those regulations is to spend a while every day checking up on a few terms and spot if there are any specific guidelines they check. For instance, within the worldwide 'fine,' there can be a 'y,' but at the way to be modified to 'i' whilst you write 'friendliness.' The rule right right here is that whilst you are in conjunction with a suffix to a phrase in which the final letter is 'y,' then that allows you to be modified to an 'i,' but the rule of thumb of thumb will no longer have a observe to the suffixes that start with 'i' as an instance '-ing.' The rule works right here due to the fact the suffix right proper right here is '-ness.'

•Make a list of terms that you discover hard to spell: Everyone has some terms in their lifestyles that seem tough for them to spell. These words want now not usually be the equal for anyone. But you need to think hard and long and put together a list of these words, that you generally misspell or frequently overlook approximately the proper spelling of. These can also be phrases that aren't frequently used, so you aren't generally sure approximately their spellings. Don't worry in the occasion that they appear smooth. This isn't a competition. It is your listing made on your advantage, so the listing can contain some thing you need. This is an crucial step due to the truth you'll ought to understand what you clearly need to research.

•Prepare a list of commonly misspelled phrases: Apart out of your personal listing, make every distinctive listing that could encompass typically misspelled phrases. You can test on the internet or on YouTube and get the ones lists. You may also encounter some extended lists, and it isn't always required of you to test they all. What I am pronouncing is to maintain a take a look at of most of these phrases for your diary or mag after which undergo them every so often, so on the same time as you're pace writing, you do not make a mistake.

•Reading books will continuously assist: You should be wondering how reading comes into play at the identical time as discussing pace writing. Well, that's honestly it. Reading lets you document into your reminiscence how a selected phrase seems on paper. And the greater you have got a take a look at, the more you come across the ones words more than one times, and progressively, you will no longer make any errors because of the reality the proper form of that phrase has been registered for your mind. With time, you'll recognize that spelling is lots an awful lot less approximately how a word sounds and more about the manner it appears. And so, you're going to gain masses from studying precise types of books.

•Look out for phrase origins: Not all phrases implemented in writing have English roots.

Some of them have Roman or Greek roots as well. When you appearance up the dictionary for the beginning area of phrases, you no longer only start records them better, but it'll additionally assist you keep in mind their spelling.

•Break down the terms: The most usually misspelled words are often the ones which is probably too prolonged. If you have got the identical hassle, then the satisfactory manner to look at them is to break them down. The technique is also called chunking for the easy cause that in preference to using the complete phrase; you are breaking it down into small additives or chunks. For instance, the word 'stunning' may be damaged down and spelled as 'as-ton-ishing.' This can be accomplished with quite lots any word you have got got problem spelling.

•Play word video games: Lastly, word video games are pretty an extraordinary manner to memorize and take a look at spellings and moreover to growth your vocabulary. You can get such plenty of traditional board video games for that reason, the maximum common one being Scrabble. If you're a tech-willing man or woman, you could use numerous spell-trying out apps like Spell Tower.

•Punctuation: No piece of writing is ever whole without proper punctuation, and from time to time, the which means can also moreover even get surely reversed if you forget about approximately the right punctuation. Imagine the situation while you are speakme. Do you speak inside the equal tone all in a few unspecified time inside the future of? No, due to the reality you either take a pose or trade your tones to offer this means that to a sentence. Similarly, in case you want the readers to recognize the precise which means that of what's being conveyed, you need to use punctuation even whilst you are speed writing. For example, the sentence 'Time to devour, kids!' approach which you are telling your kids that it's time to consume. But if you bypass over the punctuation, then the sentence becomes some thing like this 'Time to eat kids!' and because of this that you need to eat the youngsters! So, do you see what a top notch impact a small comma need to make? Punctuation essentially consists of an entire variety of signs and symbols that may be used. In the above instance, you fantastic observed the significance of the comma. The comma has superb uses as well. For example, if you plan to show the reader that there can be a pause, a comma is used. If you're making a listing, even there the importance of a comma is important.

Practical Exercises for a Mapped Memory

What you maintain on your palms is the crucial thing to a ultra-modern memory. Very rapid, very accurate, very cushty. But this method is not sufficient surely to research. (Although if you just go through all of the stages of this era, you, of course, will already growth your abilties in memory, and massive). For this method to paintings 100%, it need to emerge as a addiction in case you want to art work on its very very personal, without your aware participation. Many instances, facilitating the artwork of not only memory but moreover thinking. And even as mastering in distinct regions of labor with a hologram, you could pass for a completely new approach to preserving each health and your frame no matter age-related adjustments.

So, we begin to increase a addiction. There are numerous options for a way to do that. It is better to apply they all and, if feasible, right now.

1.Write a reminiscence improvement software program application on your diary. If there can be no diary but, you apprehend what needs to be carried out. We are recording this system for three months. Indicate the date by using which variety your reminiscence must paintings like a clock. Write the way it allows you in life. We write down the range and month in a month and a 1/2 month, and severa strains (you could half of a page or an internet page) about your achievements inside the improvement of memory. Then we paint every day the putting of all timelines.

2.Write down why you need a exquisite memory: the way it permits in the look at, work, normal affairs, speaking with human beings, analyzing foreign languages, analyzing motor abilities (ten-finger typing approach, and plenty of others.)

3.Find and write down the names of well-known those who had an awesome reminiscence, and what precisely they remembered.

four.Every day we perform not unusual developmental carrying activities to amplify the skill of holographic reminiscence.

five. Outline a table of your movements in this route and mark every day the fulfillment of the plan.

6. Idealize in case you discover a like-minded person. The spirit of opposition will inspire you. Having the 2 or 3 to extend reminiscence makes it lots greater interesting.

Typical Exercises

You can use colour postcards or photos as whole-shade simulators. So, conventional sports, decided on or mainly designed for the improvement of the capability of holographic memory.

The First Exercise: Transferring Pictures to a Mental Screen

•Lay within the the the the front of you 5 to 10 gambling cards of whole-shade simulators (coloration playing playing cards).

•Having cautiously checked out the primary card (postcard), hold in thoughts it on a intellectual show display screen proper in the front of you. Then take a look at the second one card after which present it at the intellectual show. And so on, third, fourth, and all the relaxation. For lack of on hand card simulators or postcards, you can use the pics, any gadgets, honestly all which you see inside the the front of you.

•After 10–20 minutes, we present the same gambling cards at the left ray, at a distance of approximately 5 centimeters from the face.

•If you forgot some playing cards, you may peek.

The Second Exercise: Revitalizing the Icons on the Mental Screen

•Lay the enduring playing cards in a unmarried or greater rows within the the front of you. Glancing in brief at the card, we're not providing an icon on our intellectual display, however some item or perhaps a scenario from the lifestyles that this icon reminds to. Moreover, we constitute it now not best visually, but furthermore with sounds and sensations of contact.

For example, you checked out the circle icon. On the highbrow display screen, you can take delivery of as true with the terrific and comfortable solar, yourself at the beach, the sensations of sand, and the sound of the surf.

You looked at the image of the triangle. Someone will reflect onconsideration on a hill and on someone on a sleigh sliding down this hill. Someone will gift a slice of cake or cheese. Someone crusing a deliver. Moreover, we should see the whole thing in coloration and try to companion the feeling with the useful resource of using touching and listening to sounds.

An crucial detail of this exercising is the example of photos now not static but in motion.

The Third Exercise: Increase—Decrease the Image

•Carefully looking on the colour card (postcard), be given as actual with it at the left, near the face. As near as you enjoy snug. We begin to extend the photograph, making it big and big in length. Having progressed the image numerous times, we begin to lessen it nearly to the size of a thing.

The Fourth Exercise: Multiplication

•Having cautiously checked out a color card, we present the primary one on the left show display display screen, then four right now. Then 9 (putting a rectangle—three through three), then sixteen, and so forth. When we gift many pics straight away, there can be no want to in reality see all the images' statistics.

Fifth Exercise: Switching Images at the Left Ray

•Having targeted inside the the front of you 5 coloured playing playing playing cards vertically, in a column, carefully examine the number one card, which lies towards you. Imagine it on the left ray on a intellectual display screen approximately 15 centimeters from the face.

•Carefully searching at the second card, which lies a piece similarly from you than the number one, remember it on the left ray at a distance of about 20 centimeters from the face.

•After rereading the following zero.33 photograph, recall it on the left beam at a distance of about 25 centimeters from the face.

•After studying the fourth card, flip it on the left ray at a distance of approximately 30 centimeters.

•Looking at the fifth card (postcard), we gift it at the left ray at a distance of about 35 centimeters.

•We endure in thoughts in which the lightning bolt card at the left ray is, then we start scattering them mentally "prompt": photo Nº 2, then Nº four, then Nº 1, then Nº five, and so on.

In the lecture room, we begin to perform this exercising at a pace of a 2d a card. Then quicker. Each card is "grew to turn out to be on" at approximately the vicinity in which it is regular on the left ray.

Sixth Exercise: Through the Passage of Images

•We vicinity three complete-colour playing playing playing cards in a column. We switch the number one to the left beam at a distance of about 15 centimeters. The equal with the second and 0.33 gambling playing cards, putting them respectively at a distances of about 20 and 25 centimeters from the face.

•We switch on the image of the number one image, mentally see it at the hologram. We begin to bring the second one card in the direction of it, now not however seeing it, due to the fact it's miles closed through using the primary. Gradually, it'll acquire the number one one, bypass through it, and we're able to see card № 2 in the the front humans, and card № 1 will continue to be with it.

•We do the equal element in opposite order, effortlessly pushing the second card until it is yet again in the back of the primary card.

•Then we do the equal with the second and third gambling cards, after which with the third and primary.

Despite the plain simplicity of those sports activities activities, they train the easy intellectual methods very well, each for studying the holographic memory especially and for training the memory as a whole. They moreover properly useful resource our creativeness from extinction and attenuation.

Chapter 8: Successful Habits and Techniques

Turning Procrastination into Productivity

People who like procrastinating usually will be inclined to area matters off for days, although they recognise they have to had been finished days within the beyond.

What Procrastination Looks Like

Everyone places off working on subjects we don't like to do occasionally. Nobody likes making smartphone calls which may be actually going to strain us out. Who has ever heard of someone who likes washing the automobile, cleansing the residence, or doing the dishes? Most parents postpone these things occasionally, however folks who procrastinate do it all the time. And there's in which the problems start.

Procrastination can cause strain. Procrastination makes goals and plans that may be without difficulty fulfilled, fail. Plane or live performance tickets presented out earlier than procrastinators can purchase them, jobs out of place to another person who performed first, overlooked cut-off dates or trains, and masses of extra.

Why Do We Procrastinate?

There are many reasons why people procrastinate. Some people who procrastinate had authoritarian fathers and do it as a form of revolt. Other humans blame mother and father who didn't supply them enough area to loose their imaginations.

Many people think procrastinators act, expect and stay in a international of "goals and desires" whilst the rest people must deal with our responsibilities. Procrastinators have disorganized thoughts, which means they'll be forgetful and no longer able to plan subjects very well.

How We Procrastinate

Research inside the area of procrastination is fairly new, but scientists are already able to describe great kinds of procrastination. Two of the maximum commonplace are decisional and behavioral procrastination.

Decisional Procrastination

In this kind, the procrastinator postpones decision-making even as managing options or conflicts. People that exercising excessive stages of decisional procrastination are scared of making mistakes and are commonly perfectionists. They are searching for extra facts about the whole lot earlier than seeking to pick if they are able to make one in any respect.

If a procrastinator is over-knowledgeable, he/she is in risk of falling prey to a shape of self-sabotage called non-compulsory paralysis. They have countless options and revel in not able to select the right one due to the reality they may be nervous of choosing an preference that isn't best.

Behavioral Procrastination

This is a self-sabotaging approach that we ought to people blame procrastination in area of themselves. A scholar may additionally additionally get horrific grades on a check and use procrastination as an excuse. The student would possibly as an opportunity create an illusion of lack of attempt in preference to capability and blame any failure on now not having enough time.

Procrastinators commonly have self-doubt and coffee self-esteem. They additionally worry approximately how people choose the way they do matters. People who procrastinate study their self confidence thru looking at their skills. According to this not unusual revel in, if you don't forestall a challenge, your capability can't ever be judged.

Failure to carry out correctly and prolonged procrastination make a behavioral cycle at the manner to finally take over your actual way of doing matters. This will decrease your arrogance. Self-inflicted shame and degradation like this can translate into intellectual fitness problems and stress in the long run.

Steps for Change

The first actual step to exchange is your insight. The 2d step is understanding. Once taken care of, taking a path on conduct change remedy may additionally help if your procrastination is causing troubles for your relationships or your artwork. There isn't a brief, easy solution for procrastination; some thing that permits you to take enterprise steps can be useful to attain wholesome stages of vanity all over again and making you experience suitable approximately yourself.

Purpose

Why are we able to address ourselves that manner within the international? The answer seems as an opportunity sincere: "really do it" The fact is even more nuanced, and the fact that procrastination is written in our DNA is what makes it worse. Procrastination runs in the blood. It is mounted to impulsivity and regulates our conduct. Above all of that, research says that procrastination is a trait an terrific way to be with you for existence.

So, what about people who procrastinate? Are they all doomed to a life of absently searching song films on YouTube?

Great records: no, we aren't doomed. Like introverted folks who can learn how to loosen up and worriers can learn how to permit topics pass. People who procrastinate can locate techniques to assist them resist impulses and beautify their interest.

There are many faces to procrastination. It may additionally virtually be choosing pride over subject. It might be to keep away from terrible matters. Sometimes overwhelming expectations paralyze us. Don't worry, right here are some motives we procrastinate and methods to triumph over them:

Not an Urgent Task

A ultimate date for the give up of the week, a ringing smartphone or a crying baby, we take note of a few thing it's miles we've in our arms.

It is tough to prioritize matters if they aren't urgent. We all have topics that we by no means appear to do, from saving for our retirement to getting the basement organized. That's why small and big responsibilities take a seat down on the bottom of our to-do list for a long time.

Solution: Look on the Bigger Picture

Focusing on the fast-term may be annoying but is evolutionarily good sized. We suffer from a phenomenon known as temporal discounting, this means that that that we reputation on the present greater than we do inside the destiny. What we've got in our hands is the existing, and we pay more attention to it.

This remedy takes a broader angle in vicinity of focusing at the small facts. Look at each day duties from the larger photo.

If you do not have the strength to end your procedure, do now not hesitate to reconsider your alternatives. Would this change your life? What are your career desires? What is your big photo? Looking from a brand new mind-set allow you to take movement.

When you decide the proper time to achieve this, you'll face a new sort of procrastination.

Not Knowing How to Start or What Might Come Afterward

We frequently find out ourselves procrastinating due to the truth we don't understand what to do. We can enjoy compelled or overwhelmed. We don't start doing a little factor because of the reality we don't apprehend what we have to do first.

This type of procrastination isn't quite a bargain preserving off the mission however retaining off a bad emotion. Nobody likes feeling lost or useless, and this is why we watch a film in desire to cleaning the kitchen. We eliminate what we need to be doing and do something more appealing; that's what specialists name powerful procrastination. Anyone who has organized their closet or attempted limitless apparel on as opposed to doing the real art work that needs to be carried out is aware this.

Solution: Create Confusion

The important thing is to apprehend that it's far sincerely ordinary to enjoy stupid while doing some thing you haven't finished earlier than.

Create some confusion across the project reachable. Make figuring the steps your very first step. And in case you feel adore it, you can upload in your list screaming, dancing, or making your papers fly.

Some humans may additionally want every unique character's help to get better mind. You can brainstorm with a chum or coworker to figure out in which you must begin.

It is perfectly regular to particles matters up and do them over while you're getting began out out. It will most effective enjoy awful in case you expect it's awful, so cut you a few slack.

Fear of Failure

Being a piece perfectionist isn't a awful issue, having excessive necessities will enhance the first-class of your work. Sometimes having those excessive requirements can backfire. We can pass as a ways as giving up on a challenge just because we expect we can not meet our very very own requirements.

Solution: Separate Self-Worth and Performance

Procrastination goes hand in hand with perfectionism. Your high requirements aren't the great trouble protective you once more, it's a aggregate of high requirements and be given as right with that average overall performance and self-worth are associated. That blend can paralyze you.

Remember the distinction most of the individual you're and the subjects you could do. There's masses more to you than what you accomplish. Just keep in mind your knowledge, friends, passions, own family, the manner you deal with others, and the stressful conditions you have got overcome.

Working Better Under Pressure

Most dad and mom recognize a few people capable of open the textbook right earlier than a completely closing examination and nevertheless manipulate to get higher grades than others which have studied masses greater. These human beings were planning a way to examine in their personal manner. There are sorts of procrastination: lively and passive. Active procrastination consists of a few method. People who paintings properly underneath strain and who just like the adrenaline rush and focus that closing dates supply choose to start very near that cut-off date.

Passive procrastination is what maximum people reflect onconsideration on once they pay interest the phrase procrastination. They get virtually with out problems distracted thru YouTube movement pics or Twitter threads.

Apparently, selecting one or the other actually will pay off. Passive procrastination can negatively have an impact on a person's grades, however an lively procrastinator seems without a doubt extremely good, in step with a 2017 have a check. The trick is knowing ourselves. If you're a night owl and thrive in that surroundings, take preserve of a cup of espresso and open that textbook in the darkish.

Don't Want to Do It

If what desires to be finished is dull or hard, it's past due and almost weekend time, we can maximum virtually as an alternative do something else.

There are matters that no one's willing to do, for instance, if we're cushty mendacity at the bed, why need to we get up to be snug a few vicinity else? Or to perform a little component else for that depend. What can we do?

Solution: Measure and Balance

A take a look at confirmed that many university college college students who have been main procrastinators did it virtually due to the fact there had been funnier activities. They didn't see it as losing time, they honestly intended to take a look at, truely in some other 2nd.

If you want to save you procrastinating, attempt to see the large photo. Understand that it's great to be careworn on the start and bear in mind that you are extra than what you accomplish. Get to realize your self and art work in conjunction with your procrastination, no longer closer to it.

Using the Break

Not all breaks are equal. People don't generally choose a harm that benefits them. Popular breaks, which includes eating a cup of espresso or consuming a snack, can reason extra fatigue.

Many human beings choose those devices to cope with fatigue, however those breaks don't renew their strength. To make a damage be just proper for you, you want to mentally disengage from what you had been doing. Morning breaks ought to likely

168

encompass meditation, assisting a chum, or speaking to a coworker. Afternoon breaks are the most critical and want precise sports activities. The body's electricity decreases at some level within the day and breaks can re-energize you.

•Do some form of exercise. Regular workout can increase our power levels and enhance our metabolism. Most humans expect that which incorporates exercising in a workday is an excessive amount of. This is why doing longer breaks can be very powerful. Simple sporting activities could possibly encompass a motorcycle enjoy inside the park or strolling for 20 minutes.

•Naps are a famous afternoon break. Short naps may be invigorating. Many humans worry they're capable of fall asleep and sleep longer than they want to. There is a very smooth answer. It's a bit trouble known as an alarm clock.

Taking a harm may also sense like you are slacking off, but they may be very essential in your productiveness. It isn't the time you spend working; it is what you accomplish for the duration of that point. Get rid of time as a manner to degree fulfillment. You can get extra achieved even as you're taking breaks to energize yourself.

Smart Goal Setting

Accelerated Learning is all about making mastering a part of your every day lifestyles. Learning is an enduring revel in that doesn't stop even as you finish university.

We marvel at the miracles of the universe; generation is constantly advancing each day. Habits are sports we achieve this a bargain that they become a part of our subconscious. When learning turns into a addiction, it's a clean indication that we have mastered the trouble.

Why S.M.A.R.T. Matters

Learning has a few extraordinary components, from facts intake, reminiscence retention, and in fact doing. All of those factors contribute to turning into an expert, but there may be a completely remaining trouble that has truly as high significance.

Human nature favors the direction of least confrontation. If you don't gather desires, or at least have an idea of the endpoint you're looking for, you received't be nicely prompted, and you may probable nice do the naked minimum this is required. If you're not seeking to carry out a few aspect with your learning or memorizing, then what's the motive of making an try in any respect? What will preserve you centered and in test when you have one-of-a-type distractions?

Suffice it to mention, dreams can assist your learning, and in masses of instances take it to the following diploma. There is one technique in purpose placing that has tested to be heads and shoulders chiefly others. This is referred to as the SMART approach of putting goals, in which SMART is absolutely the acronym S.M.A.R.T.

S.M.A.R.T. Way Specific, Measurable, Attainable, Relevant, and Time-nice. I'll take you thru every of those factors one at a time to look how you could make extra powerful desires if you want to help your analyzing and reminiscence retention.

Specific

Let's anticipate you've got were given the intention of dropping weight. That by way of itself isn't a very unique purpose. In fact, it's so extensive and indistinct that during case you lose even one pound, you could name your purpose a success. It doesn't help with planning and steerage, and it in reality doesn't encourage you the manner a particular intention can also want to.

A higher answer proper here need to don't forget exactly what you need to accomplish, collectively with, "I need to lose fifteen pounds and in shape into the 1/3 notch of my brown leather-based-primarily based belt."

This makes your purpose actual due to the reality you've positioned various on it and a particular advantage; it's not a indistinct concept. You've positioned it handy, and now you're capable of failure. This is the reason an entire lot people don't outline our desires too actually. It's the identical aversion to a terrible response a excellent manner to inspire you and push you to collect.

You can be unique as to the whole context at the back of the aim, which would possibly encompass:

•Who is worried, if now not exquisite yourself?

•When you need to carry out this purpose

•Where this aim will rise up.

•Why you need to carry out this cause.

The final point is the most important because it solidifies a clear gain and choice for accomplishing this cause. It gives you a protracted-time period view of methods your life will exchange and might hold you targeted whilst you're caught or feeling melancholy. A clean "why" will provide you with a boost of energy due to the reality you aren't absolutely ravenous your self or consuming broccoli, you are doing it for conceitedness, to healthy into your pants, and to attract the opposite sex better. This is some issue you need to articulate at the very starting because it shapes everything else.

Chapter 9: Measurable

You want a mechanism for figuring out whether or not you have got got come to be towards your frequent goal. You have to tell whether or not there can be incremental development and if there may be a distinction from your region to begin.

With weight reduction, this is easy. You only need to step on a scale to appearance in case you are making improvement toward your aim weight. For specific goals, you want a further intention method to degree your development and the way some distance you've come.

This serves number one functions. First, seeing development is reasonably motivating and offers top notch remarks. It suggests your efforts have a payoff, and your actions can straight away have an effect in your fate. The subtext is that it motivates you to try tougher due to the truth to this point, there has been direct causation out of your actions to your intention. That's high-quality.

Second, measuring your progress maintains you accountable and on route. You can't depend upon subjective judgment due to the fact you can in all likelihood default to the course of least resistance or be able to rationalize your horrific development or widespread performance. An intention diploma like a scale will in no manner lie to you, and it will in no way swallow your lies. It will absolutely let you recognise if what's taking region is or isn't perfect enough.

Attainable

There is a exceptional line between capturing too low and too excessive. It can't be overly bold, due to the truth on the same time as you fail to adhere to that trajectory, you could emerge as demotivated. If you shoot too low, then you definitely aren't gaining plenty.

It's additionally critical to hold in thoughts what's concerned in engaging in your cause. A well reason isn't some problem that would take vicinity inside the future if other instances align. If you're driven out of your consolation region a piece and manipulate what you can manage, it is some factor that has a truly excessive hazard of materializing.

When you area the initial aim, issue out the whole thing from your control. What are you able to plausibly manipulate and control to your advantage? That without delay affects what is viable, but make sure which you aren't shooting too low to capture up on what's from your manipulate.

You also want to bear in mind the modifications required to benefit your aim, every on your surroundings and your personality. Take inventory of yourself. Let's say you want to shed pounds and you're surrounded with the aid of buddies who all eat terrible rapid food each day and don't very own a gymnasium club; what steps are essential to change your surroundings and character?

This maintains you accountable because of the truth you gained't be able to blame some thing out of doors—you have had been given sole duty for whether or not you benefit your aim.

Relevance

What is the relevance of this intention in your life, normal goals, and happiness? Why does it bear in mind and why do you need to achieve it? You want a compelling "why" because it's what is going to preserve you endorsed and heading in the proper path through the battle of accomplishing your reason. Often, we may additionally additionally have hassle articulating those due to the fact they will be tied to enhancing our emotional states, i.E. "I want to shed kilos because of the truth I revel in embarrassed and lack self notion."

If you lack an overarching cause or emotional motivation, it's instead easy to veer off the direction in your cause due to the fact there's no backlash. You received't experience you're missing out on something.

Time-Bound

You have as a way to impose a very last date for carrying out your purpose. A goal without a cut-off date is only a dream or a statement of cause. If you don't have a final date for your motive, you received't have any urgency or reason to do so nowadays in area of the following day or subsequent week. This is high to sticking to it.

If you've got an extended-term intention, it could additionally be useful to set cut-off dates for milestones inside the direction of the direction of the 12 months, so that you are privy to in which you have to be at a tremendous time. This will provide in addition check-ins to hold you responsible and impart a enjoy of urgency.

S.M.A.R.T. Isn't the handiest tenet that will help you collectively along with your goals.

First, now and again it's higher to make desires and success approximately the try, and not constantly the success. In different terms, it may be motivating at the begin to make success absolutely doing some thing in location of doing it properly. Just getting to the gymnasium and on foot for ten mins is a fulfillment. Aim for that, instead of lifting heavy weights for two hours, as might be best to 3. Effort and consistency are underrated in purpose very last touch, so make certain to praise them.

Second, your willpower to gain your purpose has limits. Think of it as a battery p.C. That runs down at the cease of the day. This approach you want to preemptively keep away from temptations and distractions and make it as smooth as viable to be able to art work in your intention. For a weight loss intention, this can suggest making it easy to eat healthily and workout thru packing your lunch, and typically having smooth gym garments, and warding off buying snacks altogether.

Third, make certain the goals you located are due to the fact you want them. Don't set dreams which can be from unique human beings, or ones which you are certain to with the useful resource of a revel in of duty or duty. You're no longer going to have a very compelling "why" to encourage yourself to achieve them, and they might be a waste of your valuable time. The greater a reason is for a person else's expectancies, the more of a chore it's going to enjoy like.

Finally, don't forget to test and display your improvement, starting from day one. Often, we are truely ignorant of incremental improvement absolutely because of the truth we can't have a look at the difference. Whatever medium is appropriate, record your self proper from the begin. You could make it visible so you can tangibly see and apprehend the distinction. The detail is to comprise encouragement because of seeing your improvement.

Exercise 1

Now that we've prolonged lengthy beyond through every element of S.M.A.R.T. Desires, permit's go through some examples to peer how they range from "awful," but in particular common, types of dreams.

Bob says, "My motive is to begin a commercial corporation!" with out a in addition rationalization. This purpose is so big that we don't even recognize what he's regarding, a incredible deal lots tons less how possibly it's far to be successful.

Let's take Bob thru the stairs and create a S.M.A.R.T. Goal for him.

•Specific: I want to open my very own lawnmower save.

•Measurable: You can measure this purpose with the aid of manner of the cash the commercial business agency makes: I will make $10,000 inside the first six months of starting my commercial organisation.

•Attainable: This is possible, but I need to lease a lawyer and accountant, ignore my own family for some time, talk to my mentor more, and exchange my time table so I can visit stores each weekend.

•Relevant: This shop represents my freedom from being an worker and hopefully will in the end fuel my retirement.

•Time-high quality: I need to signal the rent on the store itself in the next months and start promoting products one month after.

Where Bob as quick as began with "My cause is to begin a enterprise company!" he now has "My motive is to open my private lawnmower preserve interior months and make $10,000 within the first six months, and artwork for myself for the relaxation of my life."

Exercise 2

This time, you need to do it for your private. Create a SMART outline for a aim, for example "I want to shop cash."

You must customise your desires relying on your financial scenario.

www.ingramcontent.com/pod-product-compliance
Lightning Source LLC
Chambersburg PA
CBHW062138020426
42335CB00013B/1250